ITALY IS OUT

ITALY IS OUT

Mario Badagliacca with Derek Duncan

Use the QR code to access the interactive map and learn more about the stories of the people in Mario's photographs

First published 2021 by
Liverpool University Press
4 Cambridge Street
Liverpool
L69 7ZU

Copyright © 2021 Mario Badagliacca and Derek Duncan

Mario Badagliacca and Derek Duncan have asserted the right to be identified as the editors of this book in accordance with the Copyright, Designs and Patents Act 1988.

All rights reserved. No part of this book may be reproduced, stored in a retrieval system, or transmitted, in any form or by any means, electronic, mechanical, photocopying, recording, or otherwise, without the prior written permission of the publisher.

British Library Cataloguing-in-Publication data
A British Library CIP record is available

ISBN 978-1-80085-676-9

Typeset by Carnegie Book Production, Lancaster
Printed by Gomer Press

CONTENTS

ACKNOWLEDGEMENTS

Italy is Out is the outcome of an inter-continental collaboration. It is part of 'Transnationalizing Modern Languages: Mobility, Identity, and Translation in Modern Italian Cultures', a multifaceted research project funded by the Arts and Humanities Research Council under its 'Translating Cultures' theme. We are grateful for the generous support of the AHRC and for the enthusiasm of Professor Charles Forsdick, Translating Cultures' theme leader, which allowed everything to come to fruition. The book itself could not have been completed without the other team members of 'Transnationalizing Modern Languages' and we are fortunate to have had their contribution throughout.

We owe a particular debt of gratitude to all those who willingly shared their lives, stories, and boundless hospitality with Mario as he travelled across the world. The photographs in the book are themselves just a snapshot of the rich diversity of experience he encountered. They couldn't have been taken without an extensive network of people offering essential logistical support. Our thanks go to all members of the communities who took part, but especially to Francesca Amendola, Maria Domenica Arcuri, Krisha Baduge, Gianluca Gatta, Edvige Giunta, Riccardo Iorio, Alessandro Ruggera, Nancy Savoca, and Alberto Zago for making the work both possible and pleasurable. The Circolo Trevisano di La Plata and the Istituto Italiano di Cultura di Addis Ababa were endlessly welcoming in ways which exceeded our hopes.

We also wish to thank Chloe Johnson and Liverpool University Press for their support for the book. The generosity of the British Italian Society, the KE and Impact Fund at St Andrews University, and the Department of Italian Studies at the University of Durham made publication possible and is very much appreciated.

INTRODUCTORY NOTE

Mario Badagliacca and Derek Duncan

'Transnationalizing Modern Languages: Mobility, Identity and Translation in Modern Italian Cultures' (TML) was a three-year research project funded by the UK AHRC's 'Translating Cultures' initiative. The scheme's broad aim was to improve communication and understanding, and 'translation' was defined very broadly to encompass all forms of transformative movement across languages and cultures. People caught up in these movements could be seen as 'translators' skilled in the creative arts of adaptation, invention, and interpretation. TML set out to explore the types of mobility that informed modern Italian culture and the interactions of Italian migrants with other cultures. The project involved five British universities, and its team of twelve researchers looked at different aspects of Italian heritage and cultural memory across the globe in Europe, North and South America, and Africa. We were very interested in how people remembered their attachments to Italy and in how their memories were expressed, not always consciously, in their daily lives. TML was equally interested in recent migrants to Italy and in how the nation is changing through their transformative contribution to Italian culture. We knew that the questions we were asking were complex and that they would give us no simple or straightforward answers. Working with cultural associations, artists, writers, and educators we tried to get a better understanding of what migration meant for people who left Italy, their descendants and the communities they moved into. Language was an important measure of how people maintained links with Italy, but equally as important were food, music, architecture, religion, and countless other ways of 'being Italian' – whatever that meant in the places people moved to and made new lives.

We were interested in finding the best ways in which to tell migrations stories in all their diversity. Mario Badagliacca joined TML as its artist in residence to explore the same questions as the other researchers but in a different medium. His ongoing involvement with the Archive of Migrant Memories in Rome and his photographic work on the island of Lampedusa and in immigrant detention centres proved invaluable resources for understanding the diversity of the migrant experience and the complex subjectivity of people who move. *Italy is Out* represents Mario's contribution to TML's investigation into Italians and Italian culture abroad. His portraits shot in Argentina, England, Ethiopia, Tunisia, and the US are accompanied in this book by a series of short essays written by members of the research team or by people who were involved in some way with the project. Some of the essays place Mario's portraits in the historical context of diaspora and colonialism, some comment on the photographs themselves, and some reflect more creatively or personally on what migration means. The variety of these voices and how they speak characterizes TML's ongoing fascination with migration stories and the many ways in which they need to be told.

The work Mario produced for *Italy is Out* formed part of TML's end of project exhibitions at the British School at Rome, and the Italian Cultural Institute in London in 2016, and in Melbourne, New York, and Tunis in 2017. Solo exhibitions of the work have been held in Columbus (Ohio), Venice, Liverpool, and Perth (Scotland). The work is now part of the permanent collection at the Hopkins Hall Gallery in Columbus. Mario has also lectured internationally on this project and his work as a photographer. More information about the range of Mario's portfolio can be found on his website: www.mariobadagliacca.com.

Full details about TML and the research team (Charles Burdett, Jennifer Burns, Jacopo Colombini, Derek Duncan, Margaret Hills de Zárate, Luisa Percopo, Carlo Pirozzi, Loredana Polezzi, Barbara Spadaro, Marco Santello, Georgia Wall, Naomi Wells) can be found on our website: www.transnationalmodernlanguages.ac.uk.

MYTH PROPOSES

Mario Badagliacca

Myth proposes, action disposes
(Bruce Chatwin, *Songlines*)

Over the last few years, I have been working on borders (in the broadest sense of the term) and on documenting migration to Italy. First as a political activist and student interested in migration, then as a photographer, I have been looking in particular at people who cross the Mediterranean and at the ways in which, over the years, migrant communities have settled in Italy. In 2014, Derek Duncan invited me to take part in the *Being Human Festival* at St Andrews University with an exhibition of *Lettere dal CIE*, a series of black and white photographs I had taken in Italy's immigration removal centres (as they are currently called in the UK). About a year later, Derek asked me to join the TML project as artist in residence. He wanted me to explore what Italian identity or *Italianità* meant to Italians living abroad. I immediately said 'yes', giving him the idea that everything was under control and I knew exactly what I was going to do. When I put the phone down, I realized that I didn't have the first idea about how to develop a concept as complex as culture (or cultures) through photography. Other than thinking that TML might be setting me a trap, the only thing I knew for sure was that I didn't want to take pictures of cooks and pizza chefs in case I ended up repeating the usual Italian stereotypes.

Food did come back later through the backdoor thanks to Julia Della Croce, chef, gastronomy journalist and activist, photographed in the US. Her idea that food can be seen as a tool of political emancipation made me realize that you can't avoid it when you're talking about Italian culture. As a result, I decided right away to make use of all the analytical tools I had and usually bring to bear on my photographic projects. For me, this means bringing together documentary photography, social sciences, and a good helping of curiosity. In effect, photography has always been a way for me to get into places where I would never have gone had I not been a photographer. In addition, I have always seen photography as a translation of reality rather than a transcription of the real. Once I admitted that I only had quite a vague knowledge of migration from Italy, I decided to come at the project from a social and historical angle, cutting across time and space, looking at three different generations of Italians abroad. The first generation comprised Italians who emigrated midway through the twentieth century and who, in many ways, represent what we imagine as the archetype or indeed stereotype of the economic migrant, the self-made man. The second group was made up of people of Italian origin who were born abroad. I was especially interested in finding out what kind of relationship you can have with your parents' or grandparents' culture when you live between two cultures and sometimes don't even speak Italian. The third category consisted of a younger generation of Italians who emigrated in the last twenty or so years, leaving behind an Italy which didn't reward ability, was in a state of economic crisis, characterized by exploitation in the workplace, and with a social, political, and economic system often dominated by the older generation and nepotism. This is where the idea to call the project *Italy is Out* came from. One of the reasons I was curious to know more about this generation was because, for Italy's ruling class, the topic is still more or less taboo. The only exception are statements from politicians who accuse those Italians who emigrated in the last few years as not being 'Italian enough', and traitors to their country. The point here is to emphasize and take advantage of the romantic myth of the self-made man who emigrated decades before, as an archetype to use, by way of contrast, against foreign migrants in Italy accused of placing a burden on welfare resources.

I started working on *Italy is Out* in three countries reflecting the work of TML (England, the US, and Argentina) and later on, after a few visits, decided to bring in Tunisia and Ethiopia as well. Tunisia is the destination of a Sicilian diaspora that sees the other shore of the Mediterranean as its natural geographical and cultural extension. Italians living in Tunisia tell stories that, during French colonial occupation, the authorities regarded Sicilians almost on the same level as Arabs. Ethiopia interested me because I wanted to understand the effects of Italian occupation in East Africa on families who had been there for generations and who had lived through major historical events such as changes of government, wars, and dictatorships both in Italy and Ethiopia. That said, even there I found Italians of the most recent generation of migrants who had moved hoping to build a new life, and people belonging to mixed Italian–Ethiopian and Italian–Eritrean families.

I decided to shoot a series of portraits of people in familiar surroundings in order to put faces to the stories. To create a greater feeling of intimacy, I asked each of the subjects to bring three personal items which, in some way, represented their link with Italian culture and their own roots. This second element is still perhaps the most surprising aspect of my work. Although I had expected family memorabilia like photos, souvenirs, things handed down by grandparents, and even items with a political dimension (for example Domenico and Filomena Maraffini's 'Communist Internationale' or Edvige Giunta's feminist records), I was taken aback when one of my subjects in Addis Ababa asked me to go and photograph his father's carpenter's bench. When I got to where the bench was stored, and saw what the thing was actually like, I understood why Alberto Di Lorenzo had asked me to go there as, for obvious reasons, he couldn't have transported a solid wood bench with a built-in saw weighing hundreds of kilos. Then again, there were also the amazing ceramics in Alfonso Campisi's house in Tunis, as well as a baseball ball belonging to Riccardo Iorio, who had spent his life between Rome and Argentina and never visited the US. Baseball was brought to Anzio, his hometown, by American GIs during the Second World War. In Polizzi

Genererosa, the village where in Sicily where I grew up, we played baseball for the same reason.

In the course of the work, specific details came out linked to each individual place and life story, but there was also a common denominator binding generations and places that were quite different from each other. On the one hand there were particular events of such intensity relating to an individual's family and life experiences that would have been the envy of a character in a story by Jack London. On the other hand, there are also common motivations driven by economics and social expectations. Yet, as I met new people to photograph and went to the places they lived, whatever might have taken me back geographically or symbolically to a specific place or town of origin simply vanished. Notwithstanding the particular details of individual life experiences in very different countries, what started to become clear through the photos I was taking was that the Italian diaspora wasn't necessarily connected by things that had an obvious link to an Italy with clearly defined, nationalistic borders. Rather I was getting to know an Italian diaspora through its personal, domestic, everyday, comforting spaces and symbols.

In the end what emerged from the lengthy conversations I had with the subjects of the photographs is that migration isn't driven just by clear-cut economic reasons. There is also an idea of the journey as life experience, driven by a thirst for knowledge, that helps, just as it did for Ulysses, give form and shape to leaving, overcoming obstacles, and adapting to new environments.

MAGICAL OBJECTS:
Pictures of Italians Across the World

Nicoletta Vallorani

Julia has dark hair and red lips and smiles as she casts her eye over the table in a large kitchen. It doesn't seem strange that she is Italian nor that she writes and makes radio programmes about food. In some respects, it's what you might expect from an Italian woman living in the US. Her father was a Sardinian shepherd who emigrated to the US in the 1920s. During the Great Depression, he worked as a cowboy on ranches in the Far West making a living for as long as he could. When he went back to New York, the city where he had arrived some years before, he married Julia's mother, originally from Puglia. It's possibly not a surprise that one of Julia's favourite things is the classic cookery book, *The Talisman of Happiness,* in a valuable 1920s edition.

The pictures of Julia and her things were taken in 2016 by Mario Badagliacca as part of the research project 'Transnationalizing Modern Languages: Mobility, Identity and Translation in Modern Italian Cultures', which looked at Italian national identity outside Italy. Badagliacca's brief was to give visual form to the concept of *Italianità* or Italianness. Characteristically, Badagliacca adopted the angle or perspective of documentary or news photography with a solid historical and social basis. While he was designing the project, his plan was to avoid as much as possible stereotypical representations of Italy, like spaghetti and the mafia. Although, to be honest, you can draw on these kind of stereotypical representations as long as you radically change the way you look at them. This is precisely what Badagliacca does.

Badagliacca organized his work in three generational strands. First of all, he focussed on emigration in the early part of the twentieth century before looking at later generations, people of Italian origin born outside Italy and who didn't always have a straightforward relationship with their parents' homeland. The third group was made up of Italians who had emigrated only in the last twenty years and who obviously had very different characteristics. Perhaps because of this, their choice of memory objects was particularly interesting.

If in one sense there was an intention to identify in quite a systematic way points of similarity and difference among the three groups, the inevitable waywardness of the photographer's eye generates an even more interesting effect, playing very productively with time and space, different countries, and very varied family histories. One thing that stands out very clearly is that it is essential not to see Italian culture abroad as a single entity. This diversity has been there since the start of the twentieth century.

There are obviously some areas of cross-over. For instance, even now people migrate because they want a life for themselves that would be impossible to have in Italy and this is what stops them going back. Migration to Argentina, in particular, was often characterized by enormous financial difficulties before leaving and after arrival. Many of those who emigrated in the last twenty years have three jobs, but don't want to go back because now they envisage a future totally absent in Italy. The breaking point (truly terrible, when you think about it) is precisely that Italy is a country that delivers no hope.

Stories are always individual. The idea was to create portraits of people in familiar surroundings, allowing them to choose where to be photographed and making extensive use of horizontal planes like you find in news reporting. All this sets the scene very well. The relationship between the body and space comes to the fore, something that occurs in the course of any migration. In the photo taken in Addis Ababa in 2017, Alberto Varnero, for example, is standing in his office, self-confident and at ease in his own space. He comes from a family of builders; one of his brothers emigrated to Eritrea in 1910 and another in 1920. Alberto was born in Asmara in 1942 and went back to Italy to study engineering in Milan before returning to Ethiopia where he inherited the family business his son now runs. All the objects he chose are family photos: Alberto's father, his sons and their wives and children. Family ties give the idea of continuity.

Giorgia Giunta has only been living in Addis Ababa since 2006. She runs Fekat Circus with her partner. This cultural and artistic project has become a focal point for young people in the city. As such, Georgia isn't really part of the Italian community. She remains in between cultures, doing socially useful work. In the photo taken in 2017 she is standing, with a little smile, slightly awkward. It somehow manages to give a sense of her situation. The background is mysterious and her posture that of a young girl who seems to be walking along a border. The objects – family photos, a book about education theory, and some lengths of Italian cotton – stitch together the threads of a past that Georgia perhaps wants to carry with her. Georgia's presence is an unusual element in Italian migration to Ethiopia, which traditionally has been 'men only'. Historically, young men came (and still come) to work, leaving their family in Italy, often starting another one in Ethiopia. They have a sense of double belonging that is strengthened through family ties, with 'new' children adding to those already in Italy, unaware of their existence. It represents a sort of doubling of daily life, mirrored in bars and cafes in Addis Ababa, with white men sitting at tables and Ethiopian women at the bar.

Emigrants in the early years of the twentieth century often led very adventurous lives. Someone who really stands out is Calogero. Gaetano, his father, was a policeman in Sicily, who left Fascist Italy to join his cousin in Argentina in the 1920s when Calogero was only ten days old. In love with the law, he set off with Concetta, his wife, and worked in various jobs before setting up a pasta factory. The whole family got rich very quickly. Gaetano died when Calogero was only fourteen. Soon afterwards the factory was sold and Calogero joined the police, got married, and had a daughter. When the coup against Perón kicked off in 1955, Calogero was an officer and was involved in the surrender at the culmination of the siege at the government quarters in Mendoza. Perón's humiliation was very dangerous for Calogero and for his, by then, large family. In 1959, they left Argentina and moved to New York, starting from scratch working in a pizzeria. Badagliacca's photo taken in 2016 pictures him at home in the Bronx in a room full of stuff in front of a wall covered in photographs and CDs. Among the family photos, a portrait of Mother Teresa stands out. He is sitting on an armchair on the right of the picture. He seems as though he is about to take his leave, which in effect he will do soon after, passing away a few months after his meeting with Badagliacca. Calogero's things reflect his soul as a traveller, his cosmopolitan spirit, and his unquenched passion for photography: collections of VHS recordings, family snapshots, and the wedding ring belonging to his wife who had died a few years before.

Equally enthralling is the story of Domenico and Filomena. In the photo taken in 2016, they sit on matching armchairs against a white background. They are holding hands as if they had just fallen in love the day before. Their poses complement each other. She is upright and stiff; he is relaxed and at ease. They both have the same serene smile, their hands clasped. Domenico had first set off with his father from the Abruzzi in 1947 heading for Belgium. Both of them worked down a mine on illegal contracts, believing in the false promises of a middleman brokering cheap labour. In 1949, when Domenico was sixteen, they left for Argentina, without even knowing where that mysterious country was, joining the massive streams of Italians on the move at that time. Domenico soon settled in, becoming a communist activist during the dictatorship. Officially, he ran a mutual aid society, which the government was happy with as it had the support of the very powerful Argentine church. In reality, Domenico provided assistance to political dissidents. In 1957, Filomena was suggested as a possible wife for him on the basis of a photograph, which was in fact the photograph of a photograph. The original couldn't be sent because there wouldn't have been any other photos to send if the arrangement fell through.

Domenico agreed to the engagement and Filomena arrived in Argentina after a seventeen-day sea-crossing, aged only nineteen. They got married and, incredibly, fell in love, with Filomena even sharing her husband's political views. She soon got involved in his work and the mutual aid society became a successful joint venture. Obviously, the picture that Filomena sent Domenico is among their important objects, alongside an old suitcase containing other photographs and a copy of the 'Internationale' in Spanish.

The hardest thing to understand is the extent to which these different groups of emigrants remain tied to Italy or have become integrated in the places they moved to. For instance, Calogero went to Sicily for the first time when he was seventy-eight, after dreaming about it his entire life. He didn't like it. It didn't even resemble the 'imaginary homeland' he had dreamed of. Inevitably he was disappointed. More recent emigrants never break entirely their links with where they come from and, in different degrees, hold onto their objects in an almost fetishistic way. The pain of nostalgia has an impact on the possibilities for settling down and creates unexpected moments of solidarity and sharing. Rita Strazzera, for example, is Sicilian in origin. Her father made his fortune making fishing equipment, which was completely innovative for the time, exporting it from Sicily to Tunisia. Rita remembers French colonial occupation very vividly and how in schools in those days Tunisians and Sicilians were treated with equal contempt. This treatment made them, in a sense, 'related' and inter-marriage became more frequent.

The people in the photos deal with their feelings in different ways and, because of that, the objects that they put on display have a very dense symbolic value, particularly in certain instances. They are at the same time very important, but also slippery because of their links to a person's life, endowing them with a unique set of connotations and a subjective intensity. They are quite literally the historical memory of lived experience. Probably at other moments in their lives people would choose different objects, so in that sense time counts as much as space. For example, Riccardo graduated in Communication Studies in Rome and, in 2013, moved to La Plata, where he teaches Italian and set up an artistic, intercultural association called 'Espaghetti Beat'. In his photo, Riccardo is sitting outside on a staircase: he could be anywhere. It's the picture of a generation looking for itself in a global perspective. Riccardo has no family ties with the US, but one of his objects is a baseball ball.

When the people in the photos were asked to choose three objects that reminded them of Italy, three categories of 'things' are mentioned: things related to family, books or souvenirs, and then a third category with no obvious connection to Italy and, as such, very disorienting. Alberto Di Lorenzo, born in Addis Ababa in 1954, did his military service in Italy before returning to take over the family carpentry business. Alberto put a joiner's bench among his Italian objects. The paths of common feeling are mysterious and Badagliacca facilitates them, adapting to the time and customs of the people he photographs. They are different in each country. In Argentina, he spends a lot of time with the people he meets. Those he contacts often invite him to have a bite to eat together. A relationship is formed and, in the end, all the pictures are taken in the last couple of days but turn out perfectly. Language is a crucial factor and the question of what kind of relationship the new arrival might have with an often completely foreign tongue. In Argentina, Italians feel part of the community even when they need to learn everything; in the UK, this is less the case. Perhaps it's because English is less similar to Italian? But if that's so, how come Italians are so well-integrated in the US? The issues these questions raise are complex, and it's also true that the people in the photos have very different relationships with what might be called their 'mother tongue'. Calogero speaks perfect Italian, which he learned from the Italian community in Mendoza. Valerie Lee Di Benedetto, on the other hand, doesn't speak Italian, although she has started learning it. She remembers how it sounds because she heard her grandfather speak it with other Italians. Her family was originally from the Amalfi coast, but Valerie grew up in Clerkenwell, and her memories are all linked to there. It's an Italy which has been rebuilt, fixed in time – a memory space, made up of poetic objects.

Through his work, Badagliacca puts together a puzzle and tells the story of an identity made up of many parts, never still or fixed, only fleetingly caught in a moment of stasis. More than anything, it's all about movement.

7721

Derek Duncan

I got to know Mario through AMM (Archivio delle Memorie Migranti), a non-profit organization based in Rome, which works on a whole range of creative and archival projects with people who have migrated across the Mediterranean to Italy. AMM collaborates mostly with migrants from the former Italian colonies of Eritrea, Ethiopia, and Somalia. Their accounts of the harrowing journey to Europe create an important archive of contemporary experience, and also recall Italy's often forgotten colonial past. The group's work strongly connected to my own research at that time looking at legacies of colonialism and the largely hostile responses to migration in the 1990s. Migrants were feared and then criminalized, and the visual iconography and verbal imagery through which this social anxiety was expressed has provided the media with the grammar and vocabulary of cultural stigmatization. The not uncommon outpourings of sympathy and solidarity with the beleaguered state of these non-Italians too often reinforced the perception of their lesser humanity.

Mario himself had been involved in a project documenting the interiors of migrant detention centres in Italy, where people were held as they waited to be deported or learn the outcome of applications to remain. The CIE ('Centro di identificazione ed espulsione' or Centre for Identification and Deportation) were notoriously difficult to access and, while technically not classified as prisons, their structures, regimes of surveillance, and omnipresence of barbed wire were hostile, inhumane environments. When I first saw Mario's work I was immediately struck by an ethical and aesthetic optic that went against the grain of standard media reporting. His photographs in *Letters from the CIE* investigate the carceral architecture of these detention centres and convey a deeply moving sense of their desolation. They are essays on space and the structures of man-made emptiness. Yet, while there are traces of human presence in nearly all of the images, that presence is never turned into spectacle. Only occasionally, an identifiable face. Hands communicate. Stuff lying in bare rooms are reminders of their occupants. One image shows people praying in a makeshift mosque. In another, two feet in shoes without laces frame a half-eaten bowl of pasta. Pictures on walls and hand-written messages are gestures of cultural belonging. One image shows an ID card in close-up. The card belongs to Lassaad Jelassi who had been living in Italy for some twenty-five years before his detention. He is also the central figure of a ten-minute multimedia video shot by Mario in which he writes and simultaneously reads an account of his arrest and imprisonment. The film begins with an extreme close-up of Lassaad's blinking eyes and then cuts to a shot of his hand caught in the act of writing. We watch him write and his voice-over delivered in Italian accompanies a series of black and white still images infused with tracks from the album *Ghosts I-IV* by the American band Nine Inch Nails. These memory-images, many of which are familiar from *Letters from the CIE*, frame Lassaad's story as he details what he finds in the detention centre. The ID card issued by the centre displays the number 7721 above his name. In the centre, Lassaad is that number. He makes a parallel between the centre and Nazi concentration camps, the Lager. His fellow inmates seem barely alive, like Zombies, he says. Bodies protest. Thirteen men sew their lips together. Many self-harm or go on hunger strike. We hear women's voices contest (in English) their maltreatment in living spaces they decorated with colourful murals. These acts of resistance belie the devastation of the detainees. A sequence of still portraits give dignity to faces whose lives are often calculated as statistics by government and media. The video's final sequence is a thirty-second shot of Lassaad in semi-close-up. He looks directly at the camera. He blinks occasionally, staring impassively, an invitation to meet his gaze and recognize that he has remained human. This shot is in colour.

Around the same time, Mario was also working on a related project, titled *Fragments*, a series of photographs of things recovered from shipwrecked boats or washed up on beaches on the island of Lampedusa. These battered objects bear the scars of their journeys. These lost things contain traces of their owners' intentions, the choices, however constrained, made in hopeful, perhaps fearful, preparation for their journeys. Who they belonged to remains unknown but, shot in isolation against a white background, each object speaks and bears witness.

In their composition, the photographs of people and their things in *Italy is Out* recall Mario's previous work. When he exhibited a selection of black and white images from *Letters from the CIE* at St Andrews University in November 2014 as part of the national Being Human Festival, Monica Bandella and Zakaria Mohamed Ali, two other members of AMM, spoke about their work collecting migrant testimonies and translating them into Italian. Translation for them was not a straightforward process of linguistic transcription, but the outcome of complex practices of self-narration in which identities and roles were assumed and exchanged. The authenticity of the single voice emerged through processes of collaboration. Some of this work, including a version of Lassaad's story, have been published online in an illustrated booklet: https://papermine.com/booklet/incontri-di-storie-giunti-scuola/. This process of communication through negotiation seems to underpin *Italy is Out* as a multi-layered, intermedial project in which the image is the outcome of shared self-narration. Mario's work, for me, is all about creating new connections through word and image. Lassaad looks like one of his global Italians. And their things that connect them emotionally to Italy look like the found objects in *Fragments* and their future, probably unrealized, promise. The images allow time and space to touch. Stories and faces of Italian emigrants bear the haunting shadows of recently arrived migrants to Italy. *Italy is Out* is a kind of family album. The resemblance is suggested less by common physical features than by the imprint of shared stories. The stories are told in different languages. Things cross borders and generations and touch Italy through memory. Photos are favoured memory objects. Often, they are pictures of the dead. Domenico and Filomena's old green suitcase full of photographs is a reliquary just like Edvige's chest, full of her grandmother's stuff. These containers align the past with the future present. People, like things, age. Mario's own photos host time in complex and not fully graspable ways. His portraits are finely calibrated and recognizable expressions of individuality and, at the same time, tiles in a shifting temporal mosaic. They are statements of presence, but perhaps say more about what lies outside their frame, and what we see refracted.

Mario's work fuses migration history and cultural translation. His meticulously composed images document, but exceed, the limits of mere information. Their framing and narrative iconography invite us to make connections. Individual stories are specific in their detail, yet their entanglements are equally compelling in the meshing layers of their histories. No journey is singular and Italy itself is an uncertain centre of gravity.

SEEING DIASPORA

Donna R. Gabaccia

Scholars debate whether the migrants who leave Italy to scatter around the world form a 'diaspora'. They measure Italy's migrants against checklists of the five, seven, or eleven required characteristics of diasporas. However, few scholars deny that migrants remember and often also maintain contacts to their original homes in Italy, at least initially. Diaspora persists as a useful concept in part because it focuses attention on migrants' understanding of home and identity, while also facilitating comparisons of their experiences across many countries. The themes of home and identity are also central to Mario Badagliacca's *Italy is Out*. Its collection of photographs of migrants and their cherished personal objects moved me to expand beyond my early interest in diasporas as social networks, in *Italy's Many Diasporas* (2000), to consider the visual dimensions of diaspora life.

A diaspora can be imagined as a wagon wheel with 'spokes' (humans' migratory paths away from the centre place of origin) and a 'rim' connecting all who have scattered from that centre. In my work, I have described Italy's emigrants maintaining material, social, and sentimental connections to a home village (the wheel centre) and to their kin and *paesani* (the rim) rather than to an abstract Italian nation or nation state. The multiplicity of Italy's village- and kin-based diasporas was further complicated by quite different dynamics of adaptation experienced by migrants in the many countries where they worked or settled. *Italy's Many Diasporas* did hold open the possibility that a more national and Italian diaspora began to emerge after Italy extended voting rights to registered Italians living abroad and as increasing numbers of descendants of Italy's emigrants in the Americas and Australia re-claimed citizenship there.

Mario Badagliacca's portraits of migrants generated fresh insights about diasporic homes and identities. First, the portraits suggested more uniformity in migrant experience across host countries than I expected to find. The portraits also highlighted ambivalence about whether migrants existed 'inside' or 'outside' the comfortable, intimate spaces where homes are created. Finally, the personal objects migrants chose to illustrate their identities did not differ much across host societies or across time. Both younger and older migrants chose very similar personal objects for inclusion in *Italy is Out*.

Emigration inevitably raises questions about where emigrants feel safely at home. I saw in Badagliacca's photographs migrants who existed on borders separating the physical spaces understood to be private, intimate, and domestic, and more public and formal spaces dominated by nation states and societal expectations. Most migrants in *Italy is Out* are visually framed by walls with windows and doors; these openings between two spaces position the migrant as 'in-between' people. For example, when subjects were photographed inside a building – most frequently in their homes, but occasionally also in their places of work – the viewer imagines them easily moving through windows or doors into the clearly visible outside space – the street, garden, or wider neighbourhood. When portraits instead captured migrants posing outside a building, the viewer could almost always see inside, and into a store or (more often) a home. A powerful sense of the migrant existing at the border between home and wider world was present in almost all the portraits in *Italy is Out*, regardless of where and in which country they were taken. Home seemed always in view, but never closed off. Even when posed in a still photo, migrants seemed about to move from one space to another.

With very few exceptions, I found it difficult to know from the visual evidence alone where and in which host country migrants lived. Only the written captions distinguish migrants living in London or Cambridge, in England; in the New York area, in the US; in La Plata, Ensenada, or Berisso, in Argentina; in Addis Ababa, in Ethiopia; or in Tunis, Manouba, or La Marsa, in Tunisia. Without those captions, migrants' more precise locations cannot easily be fixed by visual markers. One possible exception was the pronounced presence of ceramics in the Tunisia portraits. The considerable variations of migrant adaptation in diverse host societies emphasized in *Italy's Many Diasporas* almost disappears from view as a result. The absence of identifiable markers of the host nations reinforced the photographic framing of migrants at the juncture of home and wider world as a universal diasporic experience.

Finally, whether they had been chosen by long-ago or recent migrants from Italy, the photographs of personally meaningful objects included in the exhibit suggested that Italy's contemporary diasporas are as fragmented by local and family ties as earlier diasporas. Across host societies, chosen objects represented the continuing importance of family (photographs, albums, gifts, mementos, and jewellery), of domesticity (especially culinary tools), of specific *paesi* (the local piazza, house, street, or church), and of the Italian language (whether in written form or, in one case, in popular musical culture). In short, it was humble symbols – and not the flags of the Italian state, photographs or postcards of the national capital in Rome, or monuments representing Italian citizenship, belonging, or emigration – that summed up migrants' continuing connections to Italy and to their persisting identification with *Italianità*. Of course, one finds a few exceptions. Speaking dialect (often associated with origin in a particular locale in Italy) is not much in evidence in a visual diaspora. And photos of an official birth certificate, a passport, and a hat recalling a man's Italian military service all referred quite directly to the importance of the Italian nation state as an occasional focus for identity. Still, these exceptions, in the hackneyed phrase, serve mainly to prove the broader rule. Notions of home and identity in diaspora remain deeply private, familial, and domestic, and they continue to work against the formation of a single or powerfully national Italian diaspora even in our own times.

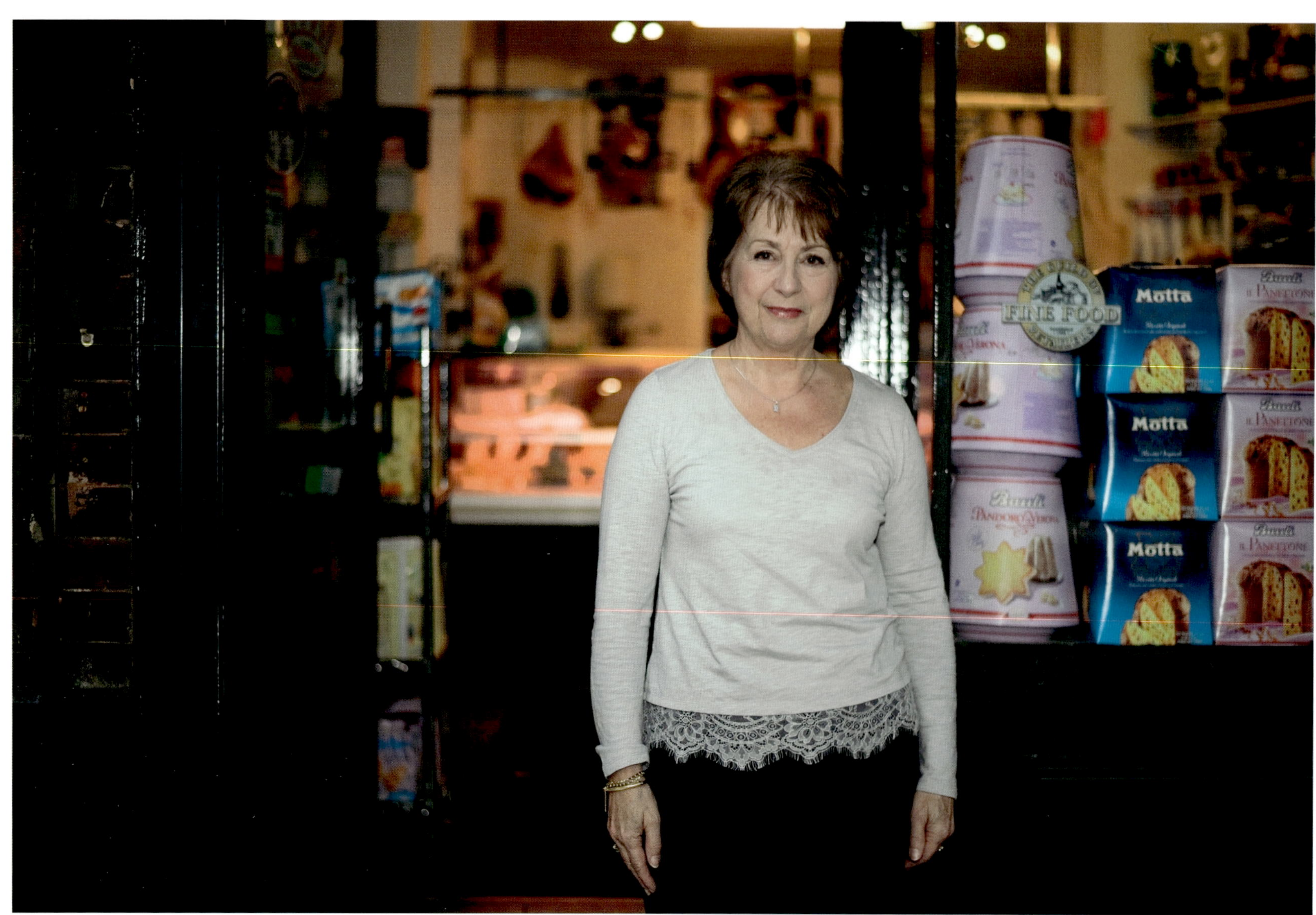

Valerie Lee Di Benedetto's family is originally from the Amalfi Coast, her paternal grandparents came from Atrani and Ravello, near Salerno. Valerie grew up in London not far from Clerkenwell and her memories are linked to everyday life and specific places. She remembers her grandfather, 'Nonno', speaking Italian with his friends in the local area, her grandmother in the kitchen preparing pasta, family celebrations and events, and holidays to the Amalfi Coast. London (UK) 2015.

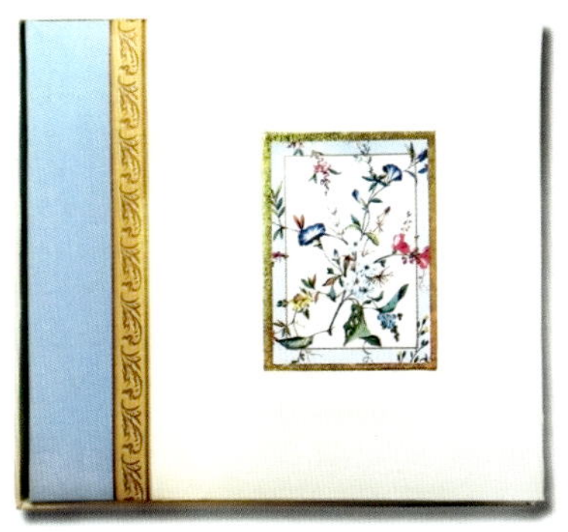

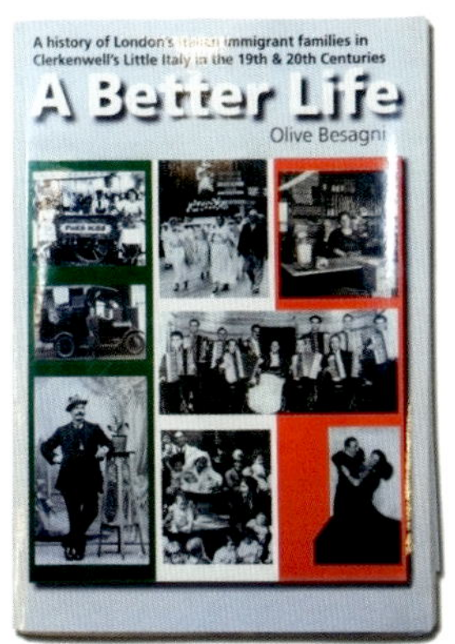

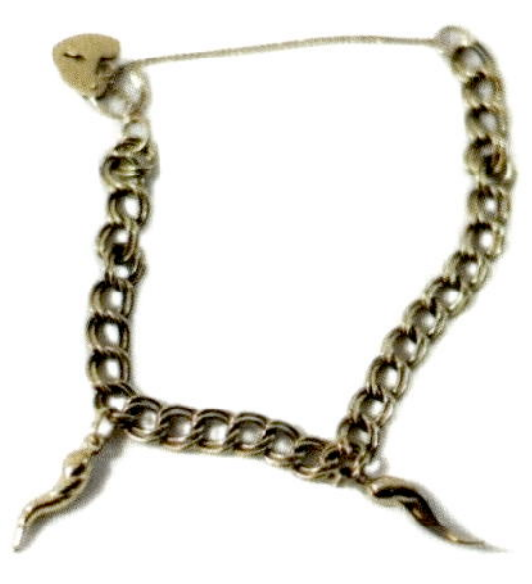

1. Family album; 2. Book about Italians in Clerkenwell where Valerie grew up; 3. Bracelet Valerie bought on one of her holidays to the Amalfi coast.

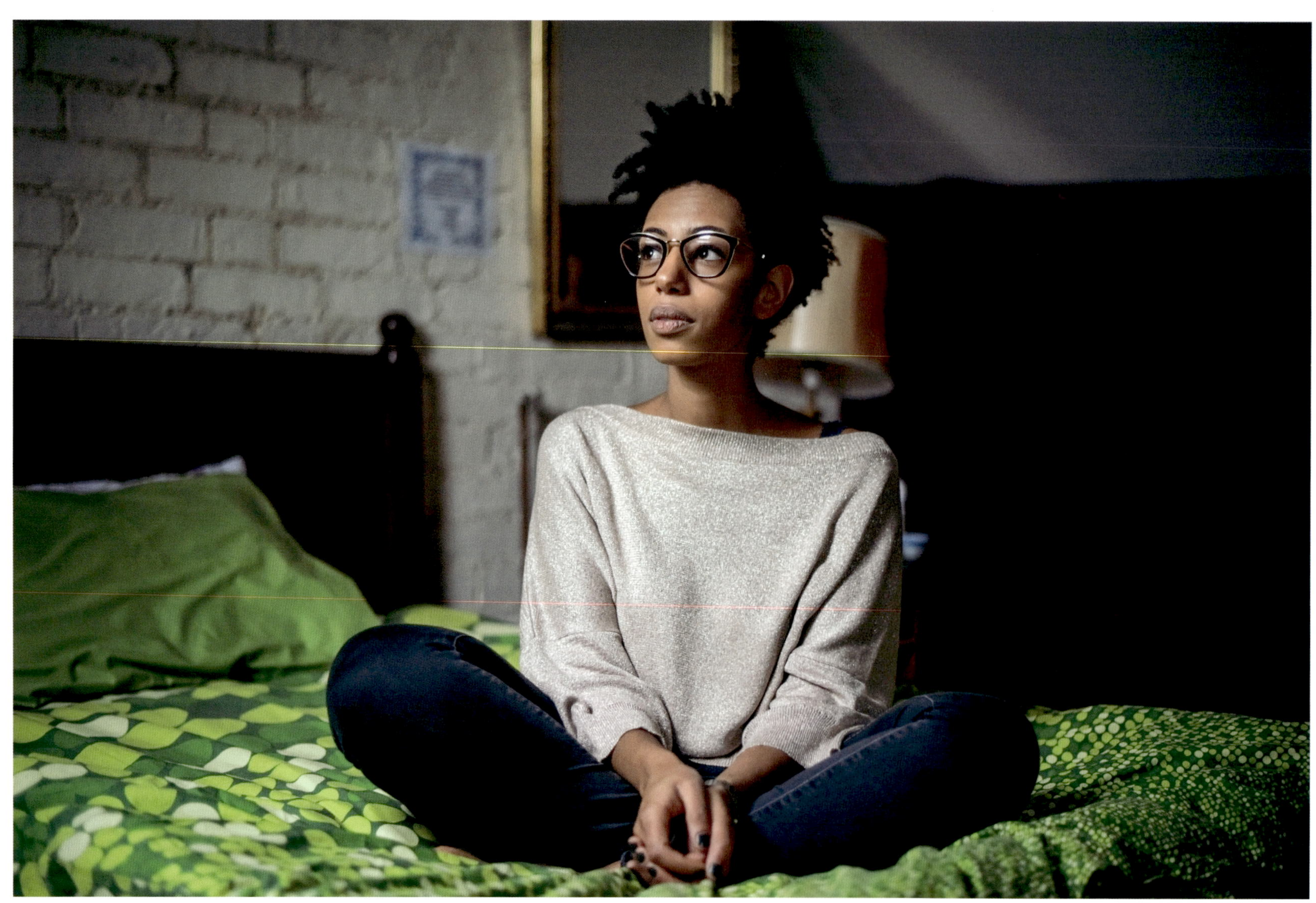

Sara Tesfai was born and grew up in Florence. After graduating in Economics, she moved to Cambridge where she has lived since 2014: 'Italy, Florence, represent home for me, my culture and everything that is most familiar. At the same time, though, I don't feel like I belong in only one place – rather, I'm surprised by the many places that make me feel at home. England is one of these. I myself am a balance of different cultures'. Cambridge (UK) 2015.

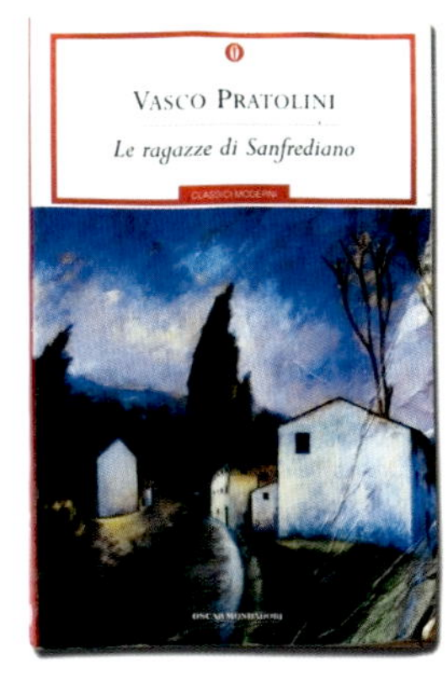

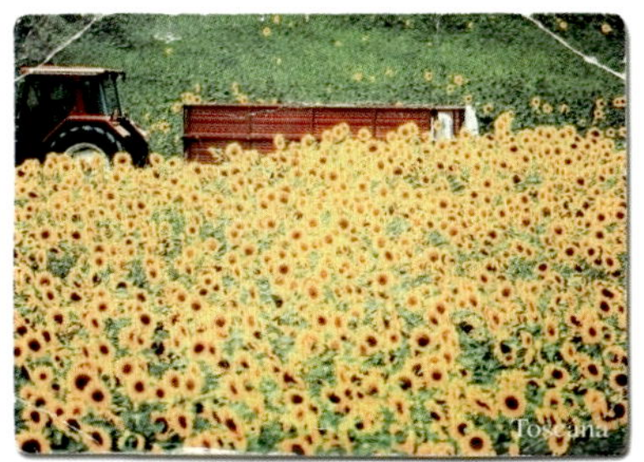

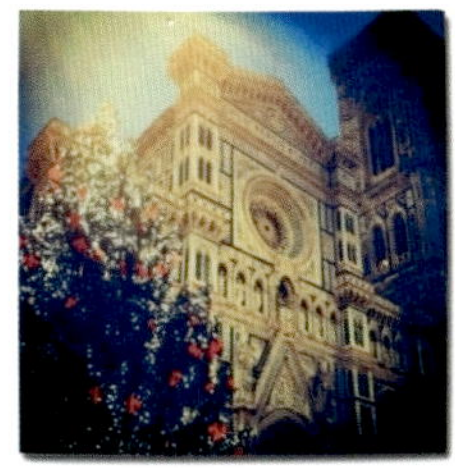

1. Vasco Pratolini, *Le ragazze di Sanfrediano*. The book is set in Florence where Sara was born and grew up; 2. and 3. Postcards from Tuscany and Florence.

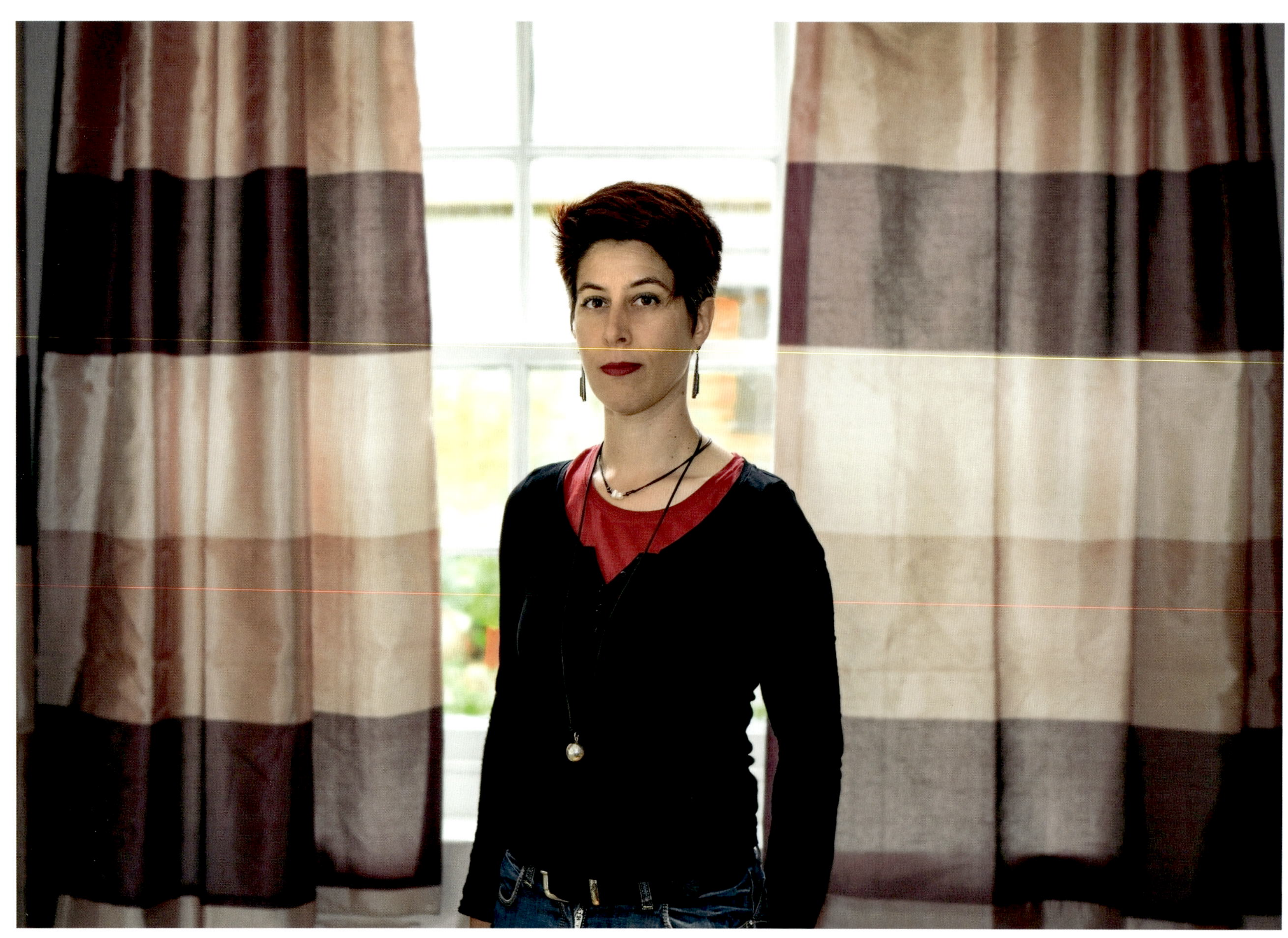

Maria Domenica Arcuri is originally from Canna (in the province of Cosenza). After living in Naples and completing a PhD in Postcolonial and Cultural Studies, she moved to London in 2012. She currently organizes Street Art tours of London's hidden corners. Hackney, London (UK) 2016.

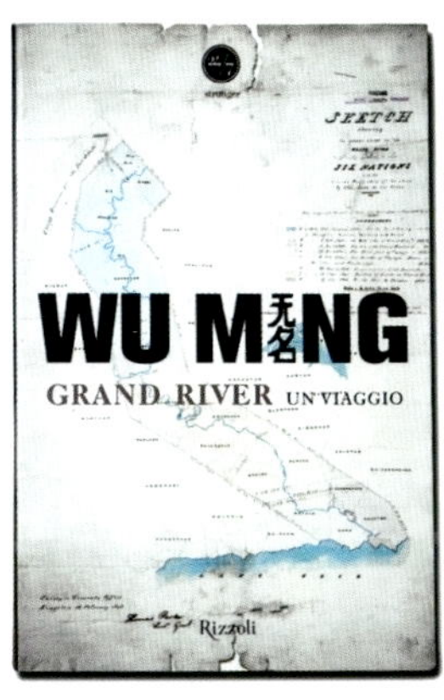

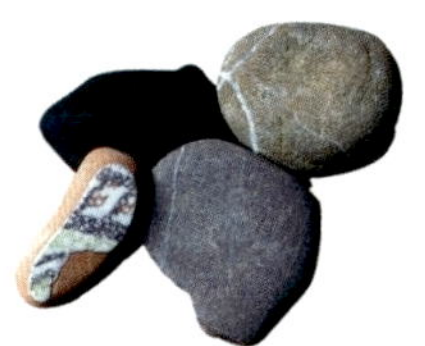

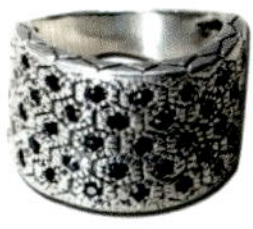

1. 'For me *Grand River* is the connection between Naples and London. I started reading it in Naples and it triggered my move to London'; 2. Pebble from Rocca Imperiale beach, a coastal town near Maria Domenica's village; 3. 'I got this ring from my mother as a present on a visit to Naples, when I still lived there. She bought it for me and on the same day I gave her a ring too'.

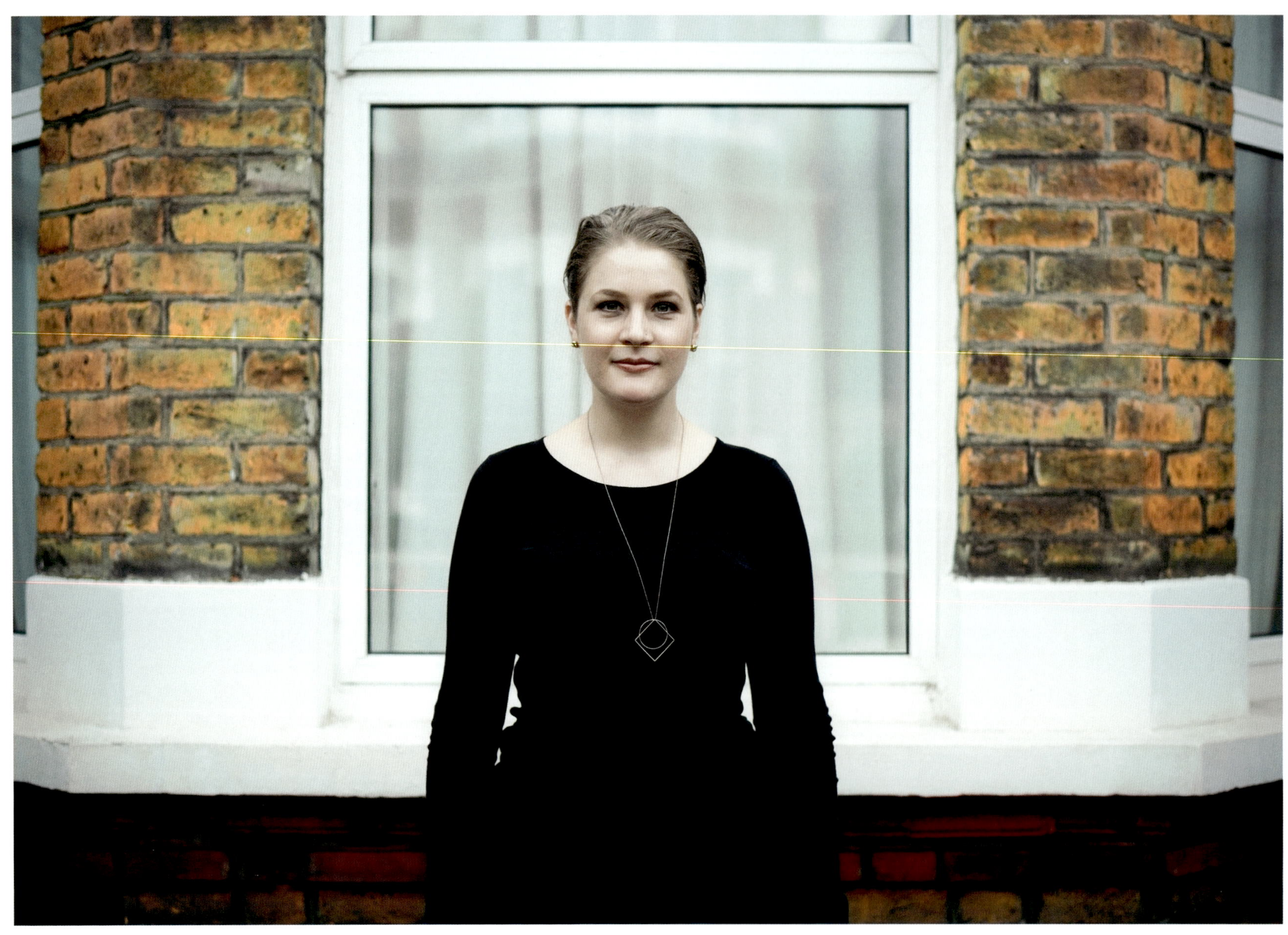

Antonia Dawes has both Campanian (Vico Equense) and English origins. She lives in London with her Senegalese husband and daughter. She had been travelling regularly between London and Naples and, for the first time in nearly a decade, was making her home mostly in one place. Brixton, London (UK) 2016.

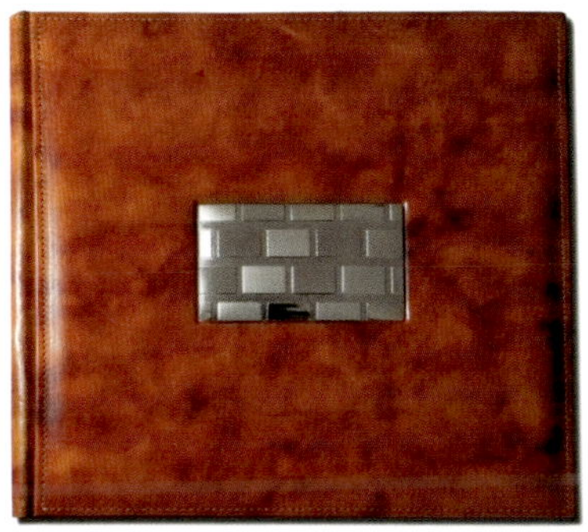

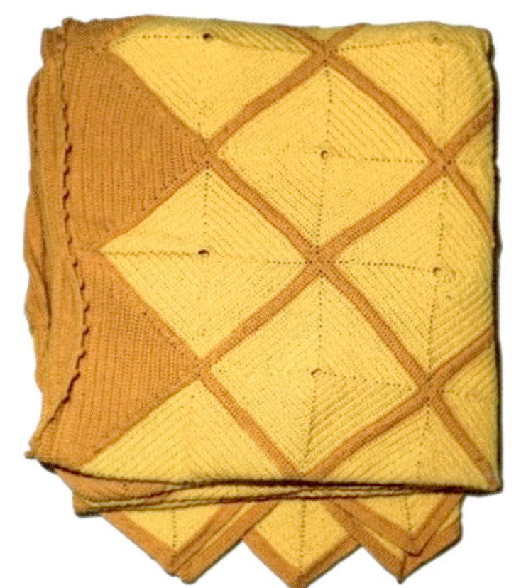

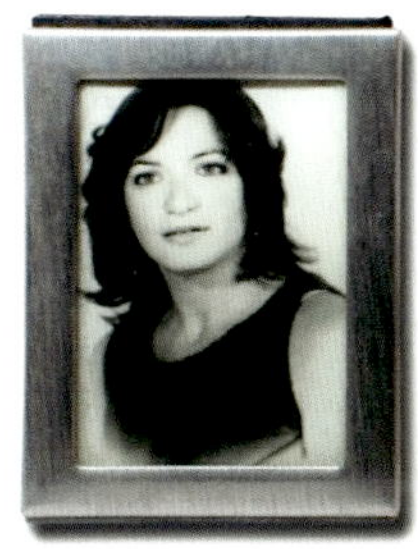

1. Wedding album; 2. Handmade crochet cover, a wedding gift made by Antonia's maternal grandmother; 3. Photo of her mother.

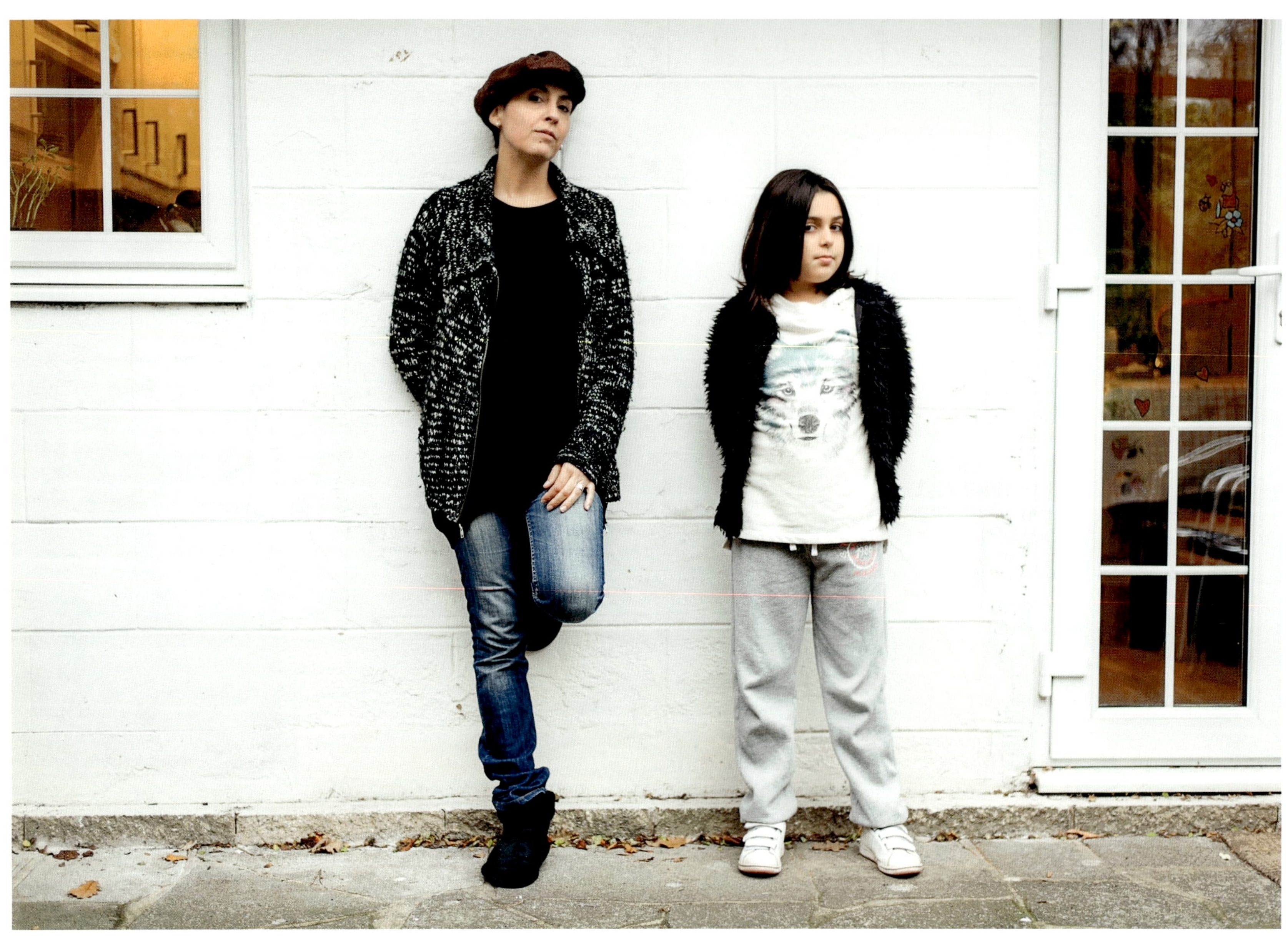

Simona and Cloe Scaduto: Simona is a photographer and artist. She moved from Palermo to London in 2013 together with her 9-year-old daughter, Cloe. Bromley, London (UK) 2015.

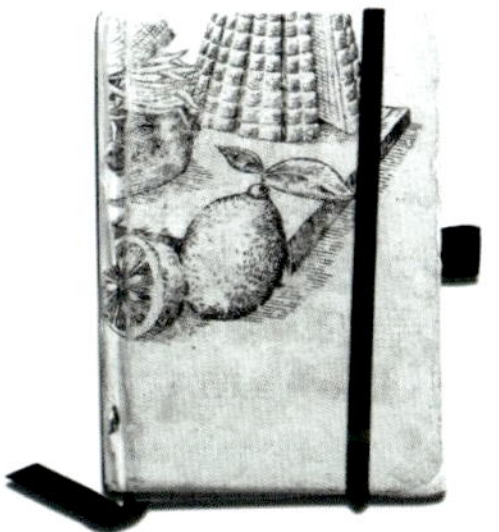

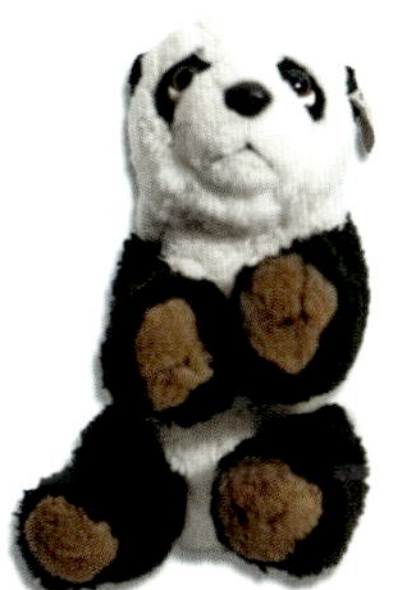

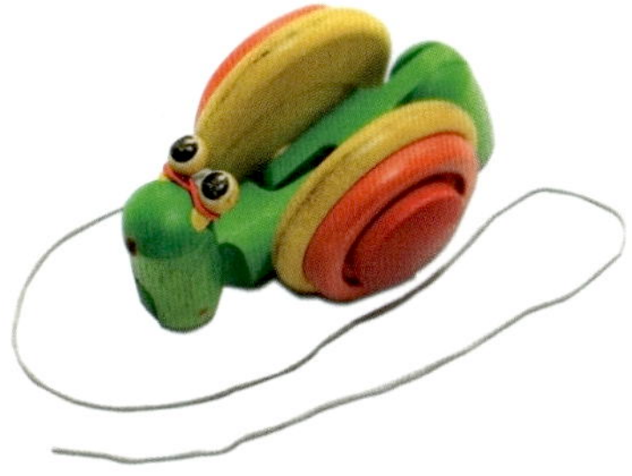

1. The diary Simona had when she left for London; 2. and 3. Cloe's favourite toys brought from Italy.

TRACCIANDO FILI DEL PASSATO

(Tracing threads of the past)

Luci Callipari-Marcuzzo

My grandparents from both sides migrated to Australia from Calabria, Italy in the 1950s. My paternal grandfather, Michele Callipari, left Italy in 1950, my grandmother, Elena Pipicelli, followed in 1951 with her five children: Giuseppe, Antonio (my father), Caterina, Bruno, and Damiano; two more children, Josephina and Michele, would be born after their arrival. My maternal grandfather, Francesco Cufari, arrived in 1951; my grandmother, Domenica Vaticano, their daughter, Anna (my mother), and son, Bruno, followed in 1954. (My uncle Antonio had arrived earlier, in January of the same year.) They left behind their two eldest married children: Giuseppe and Maria.

Like other recently arrived migrants following the Second World War, my grandparents immersed themselves in the familiar and clung to the traditions and customs of their homeland. They placed importance on maintaining cultural attributes because of the belief that, back in their place of origin, the same thing was happening. Their new sites of settlement defined their sense of Italianness, as they maintained contact with other *paesani, Calabresi,* and *Italiani*. By clinging to their culture, it was their way of preserving it.

My arts practice-led research is inspired by my Italian heritage; the work investigates, interprets, and translates the experiences of Calabrian settlers to north west Victoria in a contemporary visual art and sociological context. Through the methodology of live art performance, my work actively engages with my familial and feminine history. My research feeds my performances by inspiring the imagined histories embedded within my psyche; imagined because they are partly my concocted version of the realities lived by my grandparents, parents, relatives, and their families.

For example, *Tracciando fili del passato* (*Tracing threads of the past*), an ongoing series of live art performances, installations, and video explorations, incorporates my self-transformation into my *nonne* (grandmothers). During these enactments, I make artefacts utilizing traditional women's modes of making: sewing, embroidery, and crochet. These activities are chosen in order to highlight the significance of women's handmade craft work, which were once an important aspect of family relationships, passed from mother to daughter. The work is a manifestation of the hopes, dreams, and desires of migrant women and strives to honour their voices, which were often silenced due to the dominant gender roles within the Calabrian diaspora.

Tracing Threads of the Past: sewing (*Tracciando Fili del Passato: cucire*), a live art performance and installation, occupied the window space of the Art Vault gallery in Mildura. Dressed in character, I created a wardrobe of clothing items similar to those my own mother and grandmother made soon after their arrival in Australia in the 1950s. The items were sewn at my mother's treadle-powered Singer sewing machine. She used the machine to make most of her own and my grandmother's clothes. The objects I chose to make during my live art sewing performance were carefully considered. To remain authentic, I consulted my mother on some of the things that she and my grandmother made when they first arrived. Among the items I created were: *mutande* (underpants), *reggipetti* (bras), *sottoveste* (petticoats), *fardale* (Calabrese)/*grembiuli* (aprons), *camicia* (shirt), *gonna* (skirt), and *muccaturi* (headscarf). In my own way, I constructed an imagined 1950s immigrants' wardrobe.

The exploration and use of thread in my series of live art performances, is also rooted in memories formed as a child and young adult in the homes of my grandparents, parents, and extended families. Their homes were adorned with handmade doilies, tablecloths, towels, and bed linen, as well as items sent as gifts from Italy by relatives and *paesani*.

During another enactment of *Tracing threads of the past*, I made an apron (an essential piece of clothing favoured by my paternal grandmother, Elena). The apron was created from items collected from relatives in Italy and Australia: my great-aunt Palma, cousins Maria, Erminia, Maria, Teresa, and Carmela, and my mother Anna. All of these elements were combined in my live performance at the British School at Rome, dressed in character in my grandmother Domenica's dress, sitting at a vintage Singer sewing machine (loaned by Rome-based artist Sara Basta). One long piece of red embroidery cotton completed the apron and linked the two hand-embroidered maps of Italy and Australia I created.

As the women from my grandmothers' villages (and beyond) had done throughout time before me, collaborative opportunities to create, commune, and share together in private/public spaces also inspires me. *Tracing threads of the past: Collective Crochet* (*Collettivo Uncinetto*) – a communal live art group performative action, invited people to crochet chains of red embroidery thread, a symbol of the chain migration scheme in which many migrants (in north west Victoria especially) were participants. The collective gesture through the action of making chains of crochet in a communal setting reflects on movement and migration, and interprets the hand-crafted artefacts into transcultural exchanges of giving and receiving, sharing interwoven stories of departure and arrival.

My arts practice also integrates elements of co-creation. *Tracciando fili del passato* combined a piece of my mother Anna's hand-embroidered *biancheria* (linen), crafted during her pre-teen years in Calabria for her *corredo* before migrating to Australia. My mother began receiving instruction in embroidery from the age of nine in her hometown, Platì, Reggio Calabria. It was the expectation that all girls learn needlework from a young age. The vintage cotton fabric has become very fragile and is now literally threadbare from years of use as a pillowcase. My addition to the work included the hand-embroidered words, *'Tracciando fili del passato'* in white thread; the threads, my own and my mother's, link us to Calabria and north west Victoria. The work ties my mother and I together, and forms a dual dialogue between us, further weaving our lives together in a contemporary visual form, and has also reinstated the chain of passing down traditions from mother to daughter.

My family is at the heart of all of my research into the history of ancient and present-day Calabria. Both my grandfathers took a leap of faith in the early 1950s to move their immediate families to a place halfway across the globe, without the support of their parents and siblings, to start afresh in a strange, foreign land, without any knowledge of the English language; a prerequisite to negotiate daily life in Australia. In spite of the challenges, their new place in north west Victoria provided them with the opportunities to reward their countless hours of manual hard labour; a place that they and their families have come to accept as home.

LLAMMICU

Edvige Giunta

You and your husband devour grilled chicken between crusty, flour-dusted, ciabatta bread. Your son naps in his stroller. Your teenage daughter insists on ordering pasta from a fast-food stand that spreads unappetizing smells among displays of wooden clogs and dolls in traditional Dutch costumes. Your daughter sulks after she tastes what you resent being called 'spaghetti with tomato sauce'. She twirls the strands of the sticky mess with the fork, but does not eat.

'You were right, Mom', she says, 'OKAY?'

You hold back a self-righteous grin, shove the paper plate into the garbage bin, then get her a sandwich like yours.

You daughter knows the difference between her Sicilian grandmother's tomato sauce and yours. You follow your mother's recipe: sautée garlic, add tomatoes, a bit of water, salt and sugar, simmer for at least an hour. Your sauce is good, yet it lacks the sweet thickness of your mother's sauce. Who taught her to make sauce? Her mother or her grandmother? Remember to ask her.

When your mother visits you in the US, she cooks pots of tomato sauce, ragu, lentils, chickpeas, beans. She fries *polpette* and *cotolette*. She stores everything in recycled mayonnaise, jam, peanut butter jars that you have collected all year long. Before leaving, she packs the freezer in the basement of your American home with jars of her Sicilian food.

After she leaves, you take a jar of sauce out, hold it with both hands as you carry it upstairs, set it on the kitchen counter, and unscrew the lid with reverence.

On the plane from Amsterdam to Catania, most passengers are Dutch. Europeans like you – but not Sicilians. Tourists – not immigrants. They travel to Taormina, Agrigento, Segesta, the Aeolian islands. They go to visit the Greek ruins, the Baroque churches, to swim in the Mediterranean. What do they know of losing Sicily?

Che ne sanno?

You want to place yourself in that spiritual–emotional state you call 'going home to Sicily'. You have been doing this since 23 August 1984, the day you left for Miami. Your grandfather accompanied you to the airport in Catania. He had emigrated alone to Argentina sixty years earlier but had returned to Sicily four years later and stayed. You were leaving to study – just for a year. You never went back.

You do not like the smell of departure, its abrasive texture, its aftertaste. But it feeds you.

Nobody forced you to leave. Your parents were not destitute. You had a college degree. You could have found a job in Italy. But you felt that old urge to leave.

The plane approaches Sicily. You feel nothing. *Niente*. When the green-brown shape of the island appears beneath the plane, relief comes – with joy, excitement, and that gnawing sorrow. The process of leaving Sicily begins before you arrive.

'*La distanza è una brutta cosa*', your grandmother says. Distance is an ugly thing.

Before you left for Miami that first time, for weeks you complained of stomach cramps, nausea, diarrhoea.

'You have the symptoms of salmonella', your family physician said. 'But', he added, 'I think it's departure anxiety'.

That day in 1984, as the Alitalia plane descended, you heaved over the toilet. The blinking red light warned you back to your seat, but you stayed in the bathroom. When the plane landed, you washed your face, peered at it in the smudged mirror, did not recognize it, returned to your seat, collected your hand luggage, and walked outside to breathe American airport air for the first time.

On that first night you wrote on hotel letterhead to your parents, your grandparents, your boyfriend, your sister. You were already trying to return home.

For a while you believed you could find home in America.

Search hard. Scatter tokens of Sicily in every place you inhabit – like the clay sun that blesses the sunroom looking out on your backyard in Teaneck. Or the De Simone plate, a gift from your Sicilian college teachers that broke into hundreds of pieces, now glued together – the cracks and gaps barely show.

Bleed eggplants – with salt, to get rid of the bitterness.

Buy regional Italian cookbooks.

Fill these places you call home, all thirteen or fourteen of them in three decades, with the sounds of Italian music: Francesco De Gregori, Fabrizio De André, Teresa De Sio, Gabriella Ferri, Rosa Balistreri, Ornella Vanoni, Mina.

Shop at Jerry's Gourmet in Englewood. Argue with a worker over ricotta salata and storm out, swearing you will never go back.

Have sumptuous meals with Italian-speaking friends and friends enamoured with Italy.

Write about Italian American women authors – become one yourself.

On Washington Street, in Hoboken, meet Teresa, an old Italian lady in raggedy clothes who tells you she used to play with Frank Sinatra when they were children. Smile and think of old Sicilian women full of stories.

Watch your husband water the rose bush outside your tiny home in Jersey City and remember your father's patient, devoted, gardening.

Drive down the New Jersey Turnpike, think of Sicilian towns where the sea, sky, trees have been poisoned by fumes of factories. Believe that New Jersey is a little like Sicily.

Home is a smell. A touch. A taste. A song in your head. A gesture. The colours of the sky. *Sfumature*.

One day – you had just moved to New Jersey – you sat at a café with your husband. You sipped cappuccino that tasted nothing like Italian-bar cappuccino. For months, you had been suffering from a mysterious back pain. The left leg and foot had gone numb. You had just seen a back specialist. Your husband wondered aloud whether returning to Sicily would cure your back.

Memory is heavy. So is distance. You never arrived anywhere. You got lost on the way.

You are married, have two kids, friends, a job teaching in the language no longer foreign to you. You still chew solitude. You taste the bitterness of being uprooted. *Senza radici*.

There is no English word for your aching desire – *llammicu* – the ancient Sicilian word that conjures the yearning for something you had and lost. It spreads from your gut through every cell of you.

Llammicu nestles in the curvature of your spine, the back of your throat, the arc of your eyebrows, the middle of your chest, your tightened fists, your accent.

You wander between history and myth, memory and desire, forever a Sicilian transplant, another one who left so that she could feel compelled to return – immigrant, expatriate, traveller, exile, another one who did not learn to go home – only to leave.

Sicily never left you.

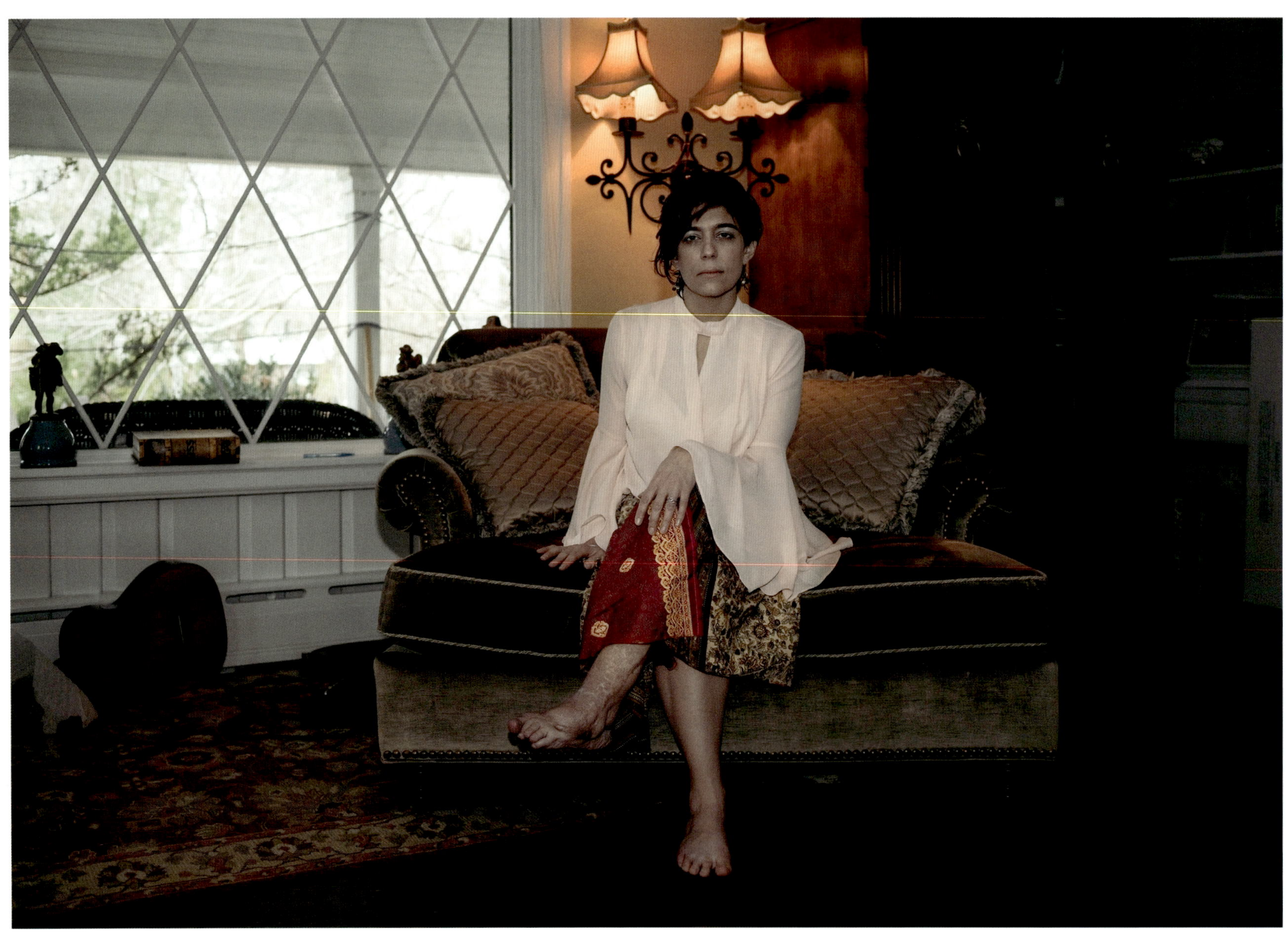

Annalisa Pastore was born in the USA. Her parents were from Mola di Bari. Annalisa's mother, Marisa, moved with her family to the USA in 1958, aged 16. She later met and married Franco, a sea captain. Annalisa is a holistic healer in a centre for integrative medicine. She lives in New Jersey with her husband, originally from Cyprus, and their three children. Harrington Park, New Jersey (USA) 2016.

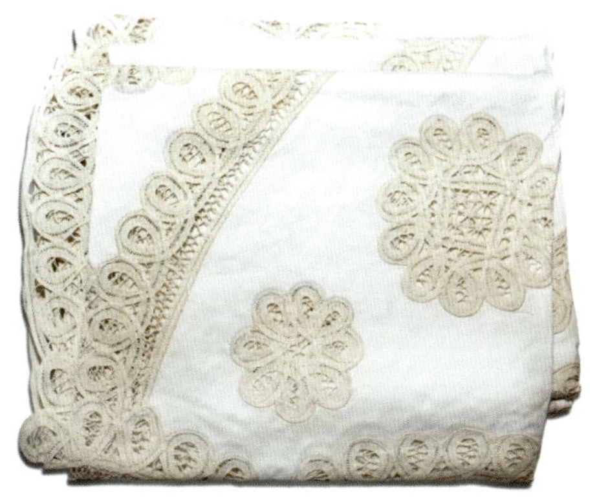
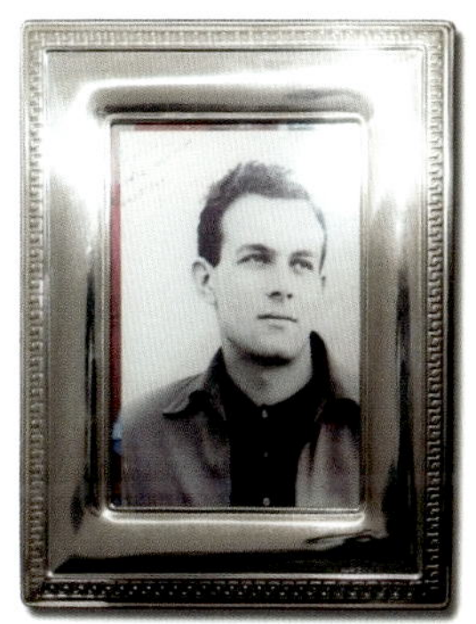
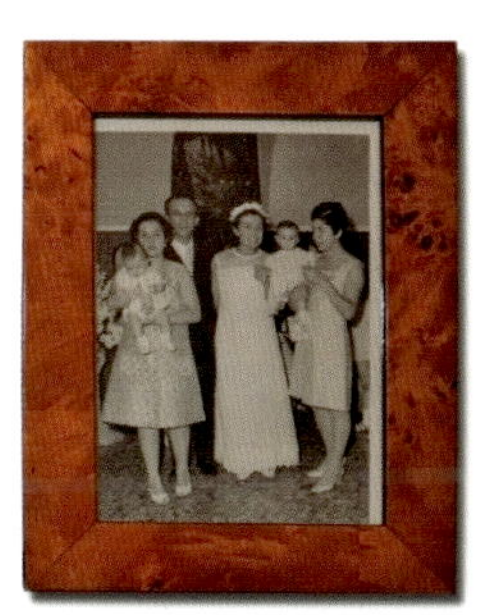
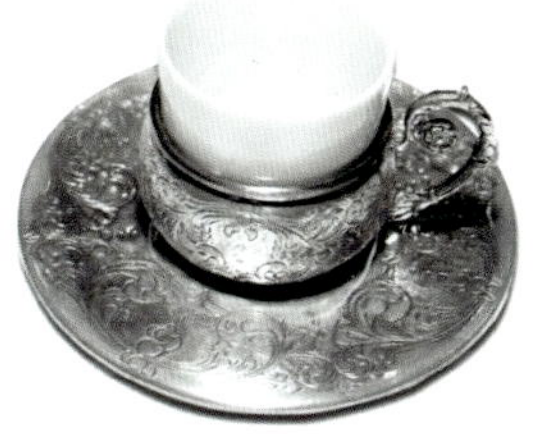

1. Sheet handmade by Annalisa's maternal grandmother; 2. Photos of her father Franco and mother on their wedding day; 3. Old family coffee cup.

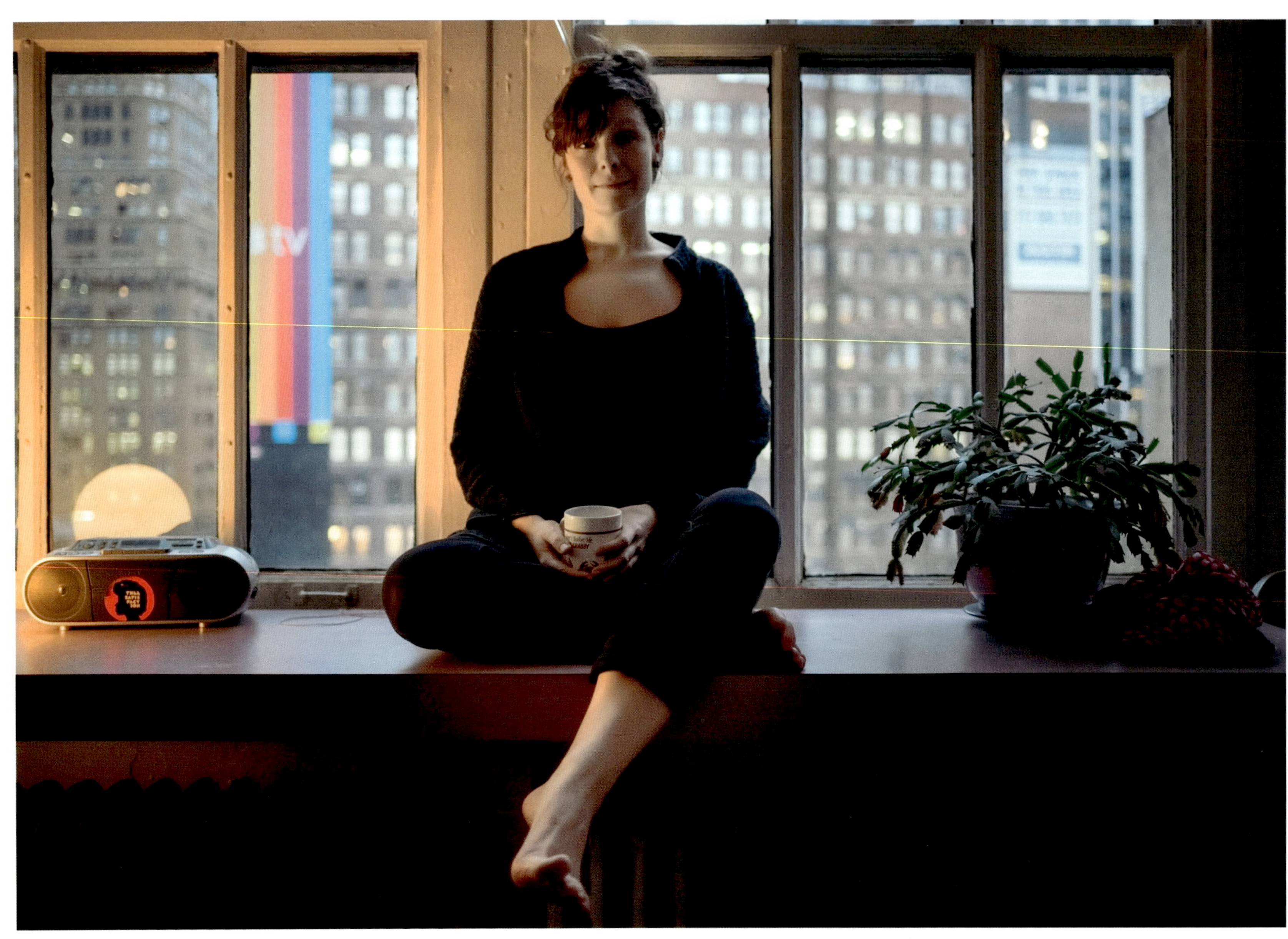

Josephine Ferorelli's father Enrico was Italian and her mother Martha is from the United States. She is a writer and illustrator, yoga instructor, and climate activist. Manhattan, New York (USA) 2016.

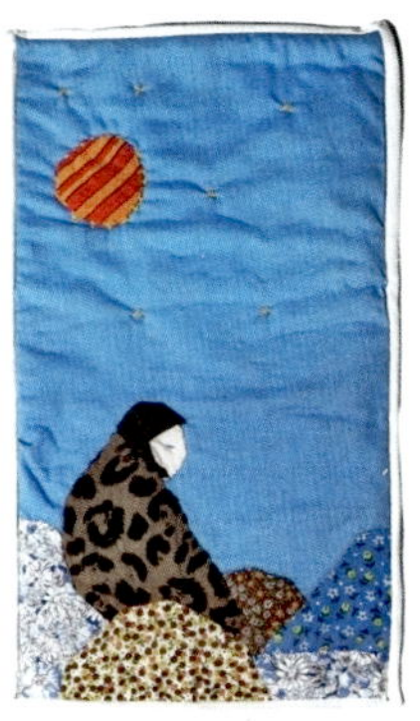

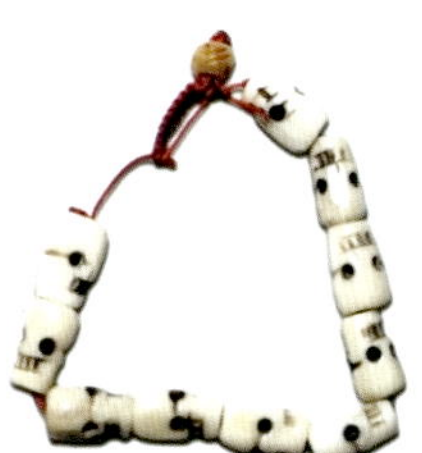

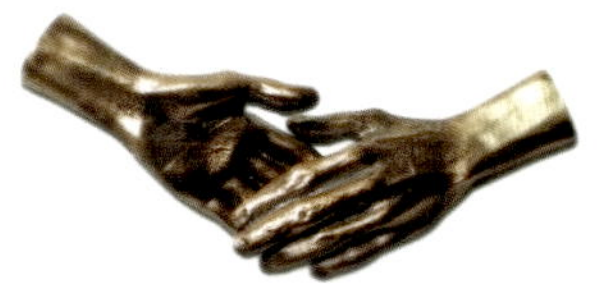

1. A patchwork wall-hanging portrait, a gift from Josephine's close friend; 2. Lucky bone-bead bracelet, a souvenir from India; 3. The hands – both left – were a present given by Josephine to her late father: 'They sat on his desk, now they sit on mine'.

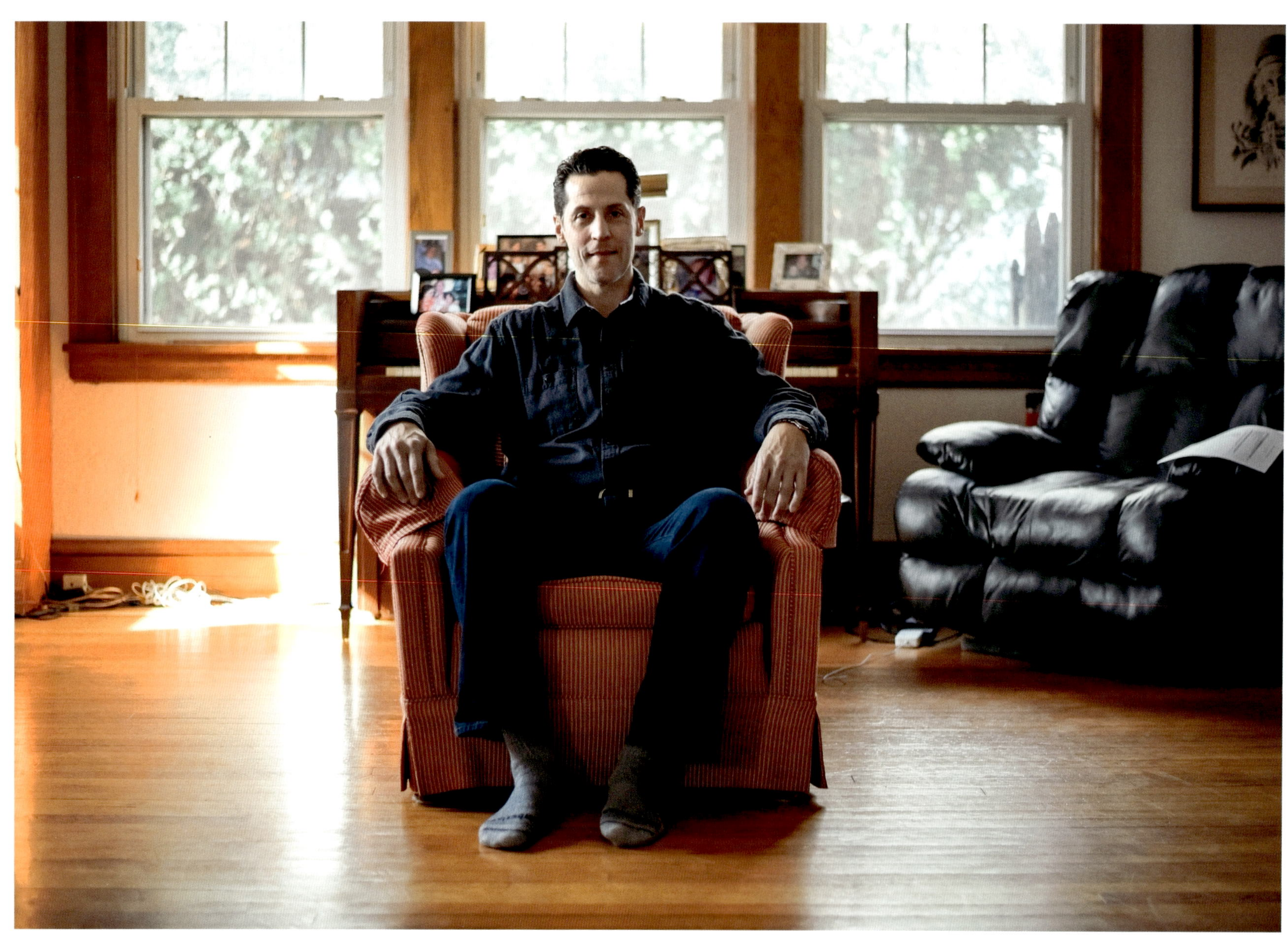

Peter Covino was born in Sturno, in the province of Avellino. His father lived and worked for many years in Venezuela; when Peter was three years old, the family moved permanently to Glen Cove, Long Island: 'We never spoke in Italian, but in Sturnese dialect, and then a lot of Spanish, because my father had lived in Venezuela and we grew up around lots of Hispanic people'. Teaneck, New Jersey (USA) 2016.

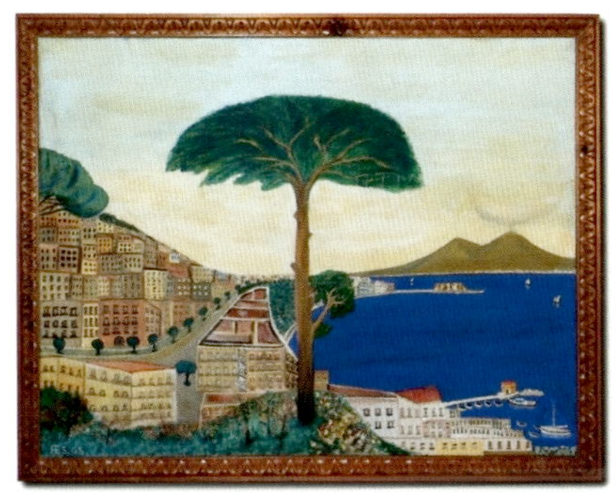

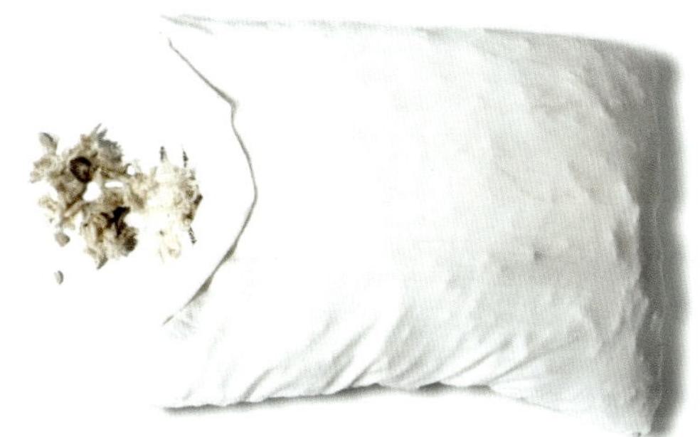

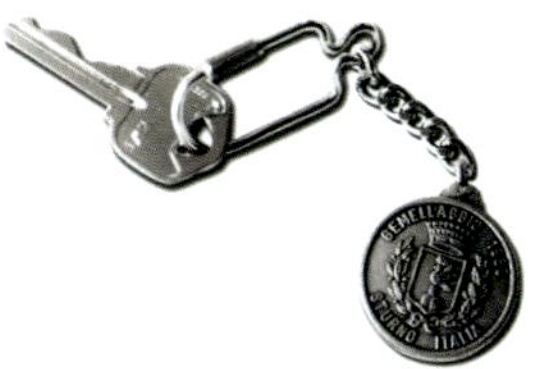

1. Picture of the Gulf of Naples; 2. Pillow stuffed with wool, made by Peter's mother; 3. Key-ring commemorating the twin cities of Sturno and Glen Cove – the town where Peter lived with his parents in the USA.

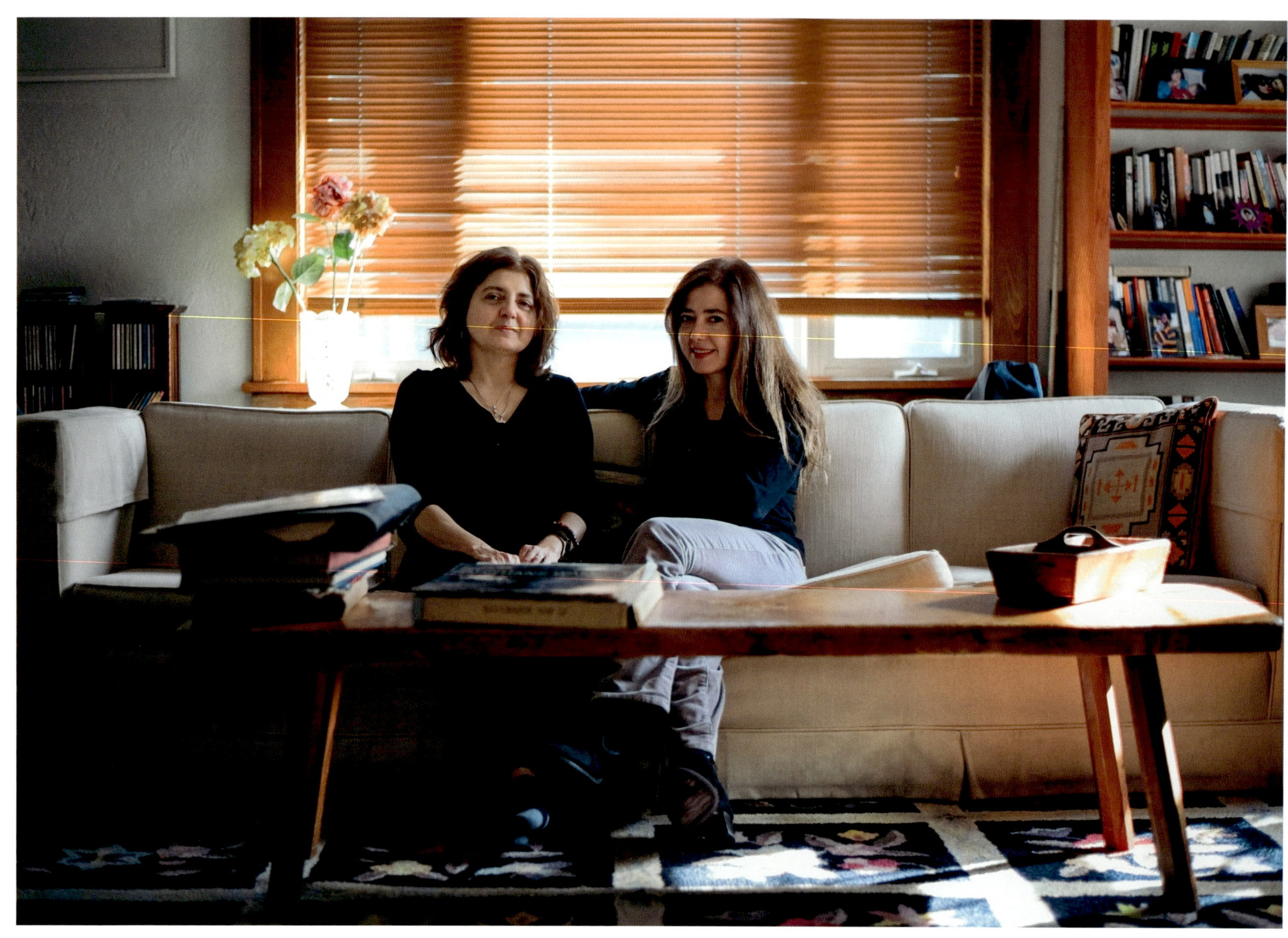

Edvige (left) and Claudia Giunta (right). Edvige is a writer and teaches creative writing at New Jersey City University. She grew up in Gela, Sicily, where she studied and was a political activist. In 1984 she moved to Miami to follow a PhD programme. In 1992 she was joined by her sister Claudia. Today, Claudia is a successful lawyer in New York. Teaneck, New Jersey (USA) 2016.

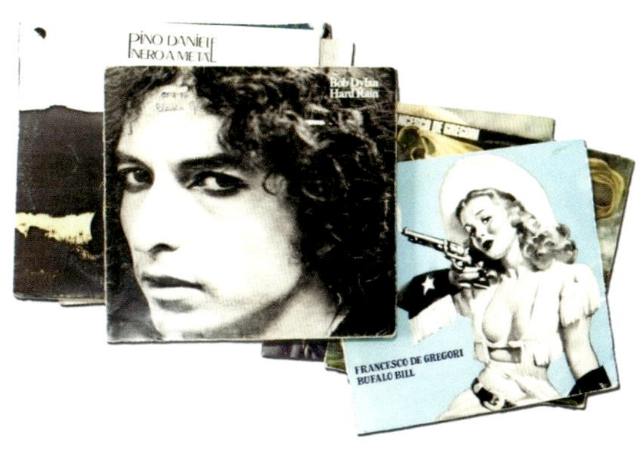

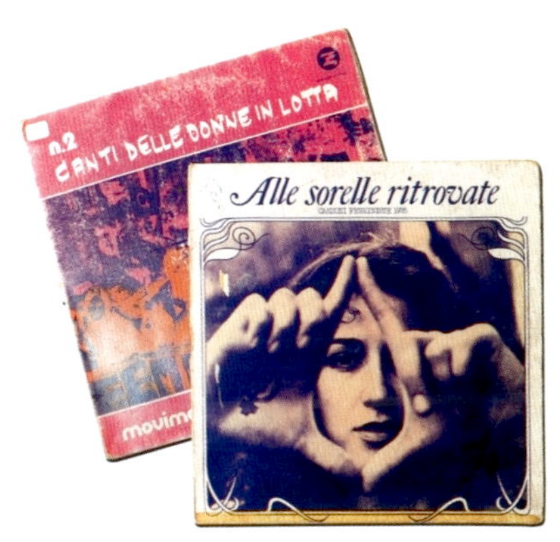

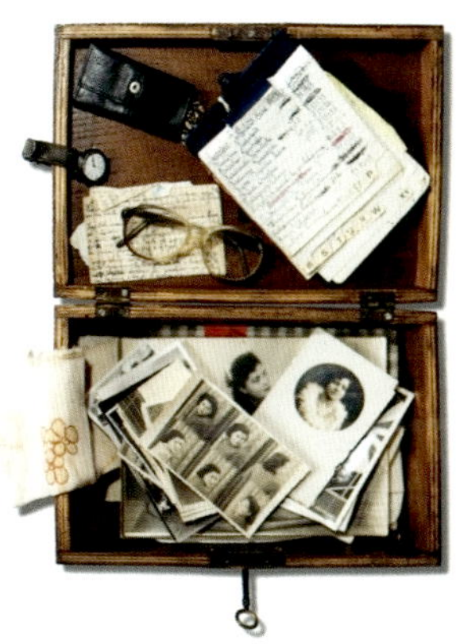

1. Claudia's LPs: 'These are the records I listened to as a child and as an adolescent in Sicily, they told me about America'; 2. Records Edvige listened to in Sicily; 3. Edvige was very close to her maternal grandmother. She keeps all her grandmother's household objects in a wooden chest.

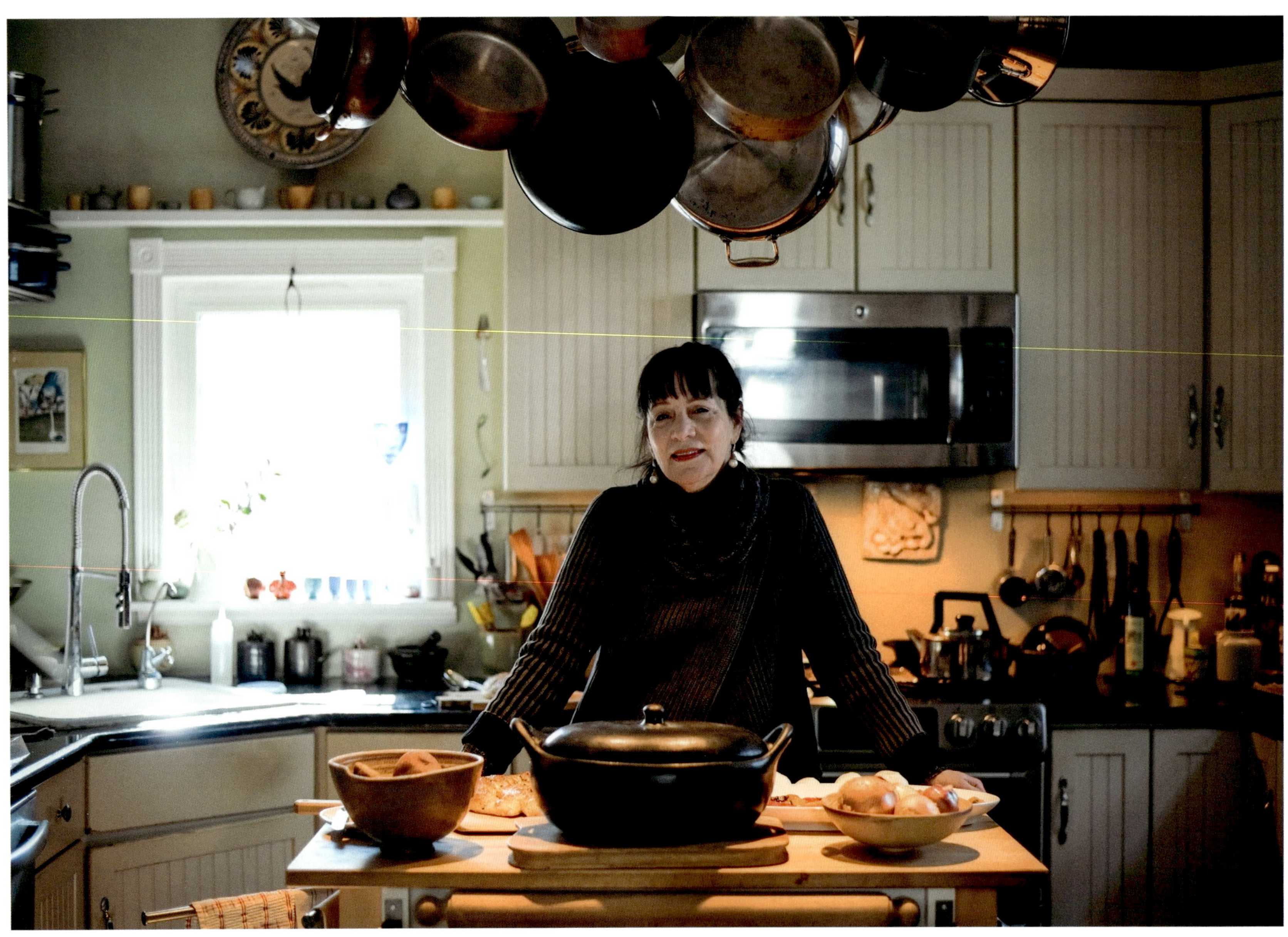

Julia della Croce is a food critic, writer, radio presenter, and journalist. She was born in the USA to Sardinian parents. Food for her is a tool of political emancipation. Today she works in food education projects in American schools, where the poorest sectors of society are more acutely affected by the excessive consumption of junk food and its related health risks. Nyack, New York State (USA) 2016.

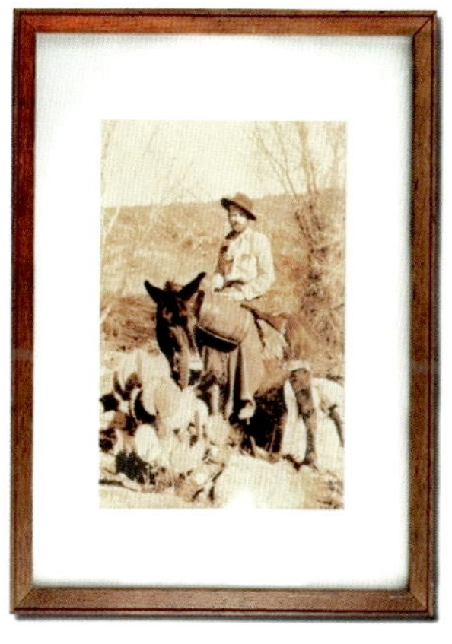

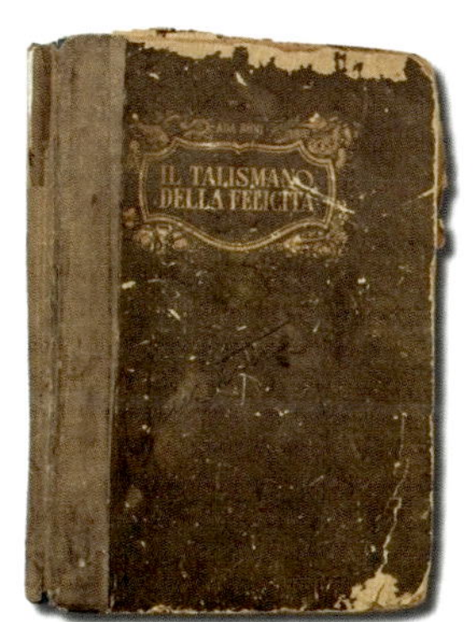

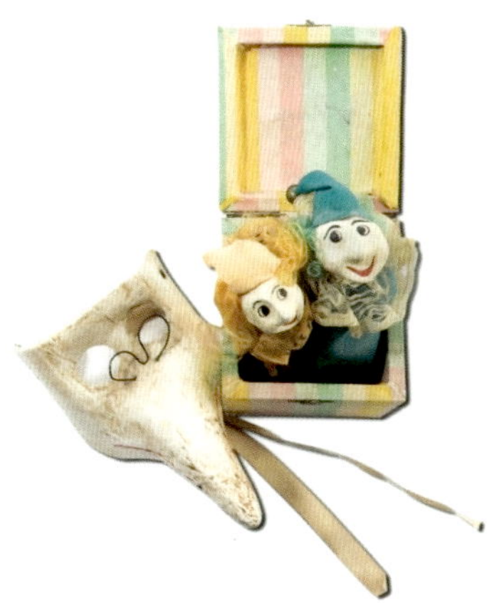

1. Photograph of Julia's father, originally from Cagliari. In the 1920s he left his job as a shepherd in Sardinia to move to New York; 2. 1920s edition of the *Talismano della Felicità*, still recognized today as one of Italy's classic cookbooks; 3. Souvenirs bought in Venice on one of her countless trips to Italy.

THE ITALIAN COMMUNITY OF ADDIS ABABA

Charles Burdett

To develop a knowledge of any location – however that space may be determined – is to become more aware of the intricacies of the workings of time. Time understood, that is, not as the linear progression of events and circumstances, but more as the entanglement of cultural, social, or economic processes; processes that are often unseen; that unfold at varying speeds according to differing imperatives; that underlie belief systems, modes of collective belonging, forms of subjectivity; and that lie beneath the ceaseless construction and reconstruction of the built environment. To look at the locations that are associated with transnational Italian cultures is one means of becoming increasingly conscious of the profundity of the entanglement of cultural practices, of the inherent instability of any humanly created border, of the pressure of ongoing mobilities and of the legacies of past forms of independently motivated or nationally sponsored kinds of movement.

Any awareness of the multi-dimensional nature of Italian mobilities must necessarily include consideration of the history of Italian involvement in East Africa. The aspiration to develop a colonial presence in the region as a whole followed shortly after Italian unification, with Italy establishing a colonial presence in Eritrea and in Somalia in the late nineteenth century. It was from these two territories that Fascist Italy launched its invasion of Ethiopia in 1935. Though the invasion was officially concluded in 1936, Italian rule was fiercely contested throughout and was to prove short-lived – ending two years into the Second World War. The history of resistance to the Italian invasion is threaded deeply into Ethiopian national consciousness, while knowledge of the role that Italy played as a colonizing power in the inter-war period needs constantly to be the subject of reflection.

The legacies of colonialism are multiple. They affect every sphere of life and, unless they are fully explored, they return to haunt the present rather than inform the development of shared futures. The establishment of an Italian community in East Africa dates from the end of the nineteenth century and the history of the community, whose composition and numbers have altered greatly over time, encompasses early colonial settlement, the acceleration of expansionism under Fascism, and the development of the history of East Africa in the latter part of the twentieth century and the early part of the twenty-first. The legacies of past episodes in this history are ingrained in memories, in representations, and in public commemorations. Within the architectural fabric of Addis Ababa and, in particular, in the Piazza district of the city, the brief period of Italian rule is still visible in buildings that were constructed at the time and that were intended to serve a purpose in the imperial design of the dictatorship. A study of the way in which these buildings have changed and been repurposed through succeeding decades is waiting to be accomplished.

Though what happened at the very height of Italian expansionism needs always to be remembered, it should be borne in mind that the relationship between Ethiopia and Italy has gone through many succeeding phases, beginning with Emperor Haile Selassie granting the Italian community permission to remain in Ethiopia in the immediate aftermath of the Second World War. Along with every other section of the population, the community has witnessed the consequences of the dramatic movement of social, cultural, and economic forces within Ethiopia's post-war history: the extremely protracted war with Eritrea, following the annexation of the country in the early 1960s, the violent imposition of the rule of the Derg beginning in the 1970s, the fall of Mengistu at the beginning of the 1990s, and the country's transition to democracy.

Within the complexities of this national and transnational context, the Italian presence in Ethiopia – inevitably linked to the nature of the relationship between Italy and East Africa – has been subject to many changes. It has declined in terms of numbers over time, its forms of association have changed, and the material evidence of its presence is less easy to detect. Members of the community tend to have strong connections in both Italy and Ethiopia and to move frequently between the two countries. Those of older generations remember vividly when, during the period in which the Derg was in power, it was not possible to do so. Many members of the community are of mixed ethnicity and, in the words of a number of the people that we interviewed, the great lesson that the community has learnt over time is not to make distinctions based on any notion of racial identity.

I was able to make, with Gianmarco Mancosu, a number of research visits to Addis Ababa between 2015 and 2017. A noticeable Italian presence has remained in certain sectors of society, for example the construction industry, while Italians employed for a determinate period of time in initiatives led by associations working in projects of developmental co-operation add to the more transitory Italian community of Addis Ababa. One of the most long-standing spaces of association is the Circolo Juventus, located behind the vast Meskel Square in the centre of the city. It was originally created in the 1950s as a meeting place for members of the Italian community, containing sporting facilities, a restaurant, bar, and spaces for events. It now serves as a place where people from a wide range of different communities and walks of life gather together, though it retains its links with the Italian community and has the distinctive feel – in its architecture, in the lay-out of its interior and in its footballing insignia – of an Italian sporting club from the post-war era.

Among the other spaces that testify to the endurance of an Italian presence in the successive phases of Ethiopia's post-war history are the Italian Cultural Institute and the Italian School that are housed in the same complex within the city's Piazza district. Part of the global network of cultural institutes, the role of the Italian Cultural Institute is both to disseminate instances of Italian cultural production and to facilitate cultural exchange at every level. In the context of exchanging and sharing memories of the past, one important example of the work of the Institute, that we were able to witness, was the hosting in October 2017 of Gabriella Ghermandi's 'Atse Tewodros Project' concert, performed by Ethiopian and Italian musicians in front of a very large audience that included members of the Ethiopian Patriots Association.

The Italian School, l'Istituto Italiano Omnicomprensivo, was founded in 1954 and moved to its current location in 1974. In offering an education delivered in Italian at nursery, primary, and secondary level to students, eighty percent of whom are of Ethiopian nationality, the school serves as a focal point for cultural and educational exchange. The teaching of Italian in the school accommodates the linguistic variety of its pupils and the school does not shy away from confronting the complexities of Italy's historical relations with Ethiopia. One of the main purposes of the school, in the words of Daniele Castellani (principal at the time we visited) is to extend for its students the range of linguistic and cultural experiences of being in the world and, by so doing, to provide one means, among many, of appreciating the transnational dimensions of culture.

One way of thinking about the present is as a shifting configuration of processes in which the layers of the past intermittently become visible. The enduring evidence of how an Italian presence continues to be entangled within contemporary Addis Ababa promotes inquiry into the legacies and the lessons of the past. When placed within the wider context of diasporic, post-colonial, and transcultural movement, it carries with it suggestions of how shared futures can be imagined.

MY BELOVED STEPMOTHER

Shirin Ramzanali Fazel

He is young – maybe in his late thirties, he has a goat's beard, dark eyes like the black olives of the Mediterranean. Behind his glasses he scrutinizes my passport carefully. Then, taken by curiosity, he asks me: '*Signora,* how long have you been an Italian citizen?'

Encouraged by his young smiling face, I reply: 'Since the time when there was still black and white television in Italy'. In my heart I thought, 'Eh, a long time before you were born. Why is it that anyone who looks like me isn't seen as Italian even if she has been here for a lifetime?'

In Italy, when I read newspapers or watch television, I don't feel represented. I feel rejected, insulted, gagged. When I hear people say: 'Italians are born, they don't become'. What an insult!

I do not deny my origins, my culture, and religion. I bring them with me; I am proud and I live them daily. The experiences of my life over the years have enriched them, modified them when necessary, intertwined them and moulded them, made them unique. I feel good in my skin. That's who I am.

I had a happy childhood. I was not aware of colonialism and Fascism. Fortunately, I grew up in an Africa where independence was celebrated. There was great enthusiasm.

At that time, I had no idea that the borders of African countries had been created and determined solely on the basis of the interests of the colonial powers. That the Europeans, the colonizers, had indoctrinated us with their language and their culture. History had been taught to us only from their point of view.

With time I realized that so many truths have been hidden, countless half-truths. The only thing that was never questioned by Europeans was their superiority. They were the model and the yardstick for the rest of the world. Mine is not a '*J'accuse*' but an observation; a burning truth that cannot be denied.

It was Italy that came to me. I found it in my hometown of Mogadishu. I was crossed by that border.

At the time my family wanted to give me the best education possible, so I went to kindergarten and elementary school in a religious institute run by missionary nuns. The Italian school was for Italians, but it also gave limited access to the offspring of a certain local elite composed of the Somali and foreign bourgeoisie, and government officials.

My parents were both Muslims, but I never heard them speak ill of the sisters or of Christians. In a predominantly Muslim country, the Cathedral of Mogadishu was erected and inaugurated in 1928, the year my mother was born. It was copied from the Cathedral of Cefalù, in the Norman Gothic style. But this was not the only place of worship for Christians in Mogadishu: there was also the Church of the Sacred Heart. Other important cities such as Merca, Brava, Chisimaio, and Baidoa also hosted Catholic churches

At school, in the Regina Elena Institute, run by the Sisters of the Consolata Missionary Order, we had a room used for prayer, complete with an altar, a tabernacle, and candles, where the nuns took us to pray, kneeling on the cold marble floor, while the smell of frangipani hovered in the air. In the garden of the institute, there was a statue of the Madonna holding the Baby Jesus. At Christmas, the nativity scene was set up and the performances were prepared. In every classroom there was a crucifix hung on the wall, at the top behind the nun's chair and, in the morning, before starting the lesson, we had to stand up, make the sign of the cross, and recite the Hail Mary.

Before we went home, the teacher used to read us aloud the parables of Jesus, the stories of his disciples, and Adam and Eve and the various prophets.

I remember how frightened I was by the nun's accusing expression when she looked at me behind those glasses on her nose as she said: 'Whoever is not baptized goes to hell!' I imagined the devil as half-man and half-beast, with horns, a long tail, and a sardonic expression on his face as he pushed sinners into the flames of hell with a pitchfork. At home I never had the courage to talk about baptism. So at home, at table, while we were having lunch, I looked at my mom and dad knowing that they too were not baptized. With each bite I swallowed my doubts and my fears.

As a child I received a great deal of conflicting stimuli and I needed time to process and filter them. Fortunately, my daily life intertwined with Islam, a religion that is also a way of life. My parents taught me that Islam is above all doing good to others. I always saw my mother helping the needy as best she could: the beggar who knocks humbly on the door, the widow with children who lives just a few steps away from us, the child struck by polio, the young mother whose son has died. Prayer, religious holidays, the neighbourhood made up of people from all walks of life – they all helped me to develop an empathic attitude towards others.

Today, unfortunately, I live in a world where Islam is demonized, and hostility to the religion has become the norm. Newspapers in Italy defame and attack all

Muslims as if they were a single monolithic mass, not differentiating them from a small group of terrorists.

The headline 'Islamic Bastards' did not appear in a provincial tabloid newspaper, but was the main headline in a national newspaper, *Libero*. The director, Maurizio Belpietro, was sued by the CAIM (Coordination of the Islamic Associations of Milan and Monza), which, in association with the public prosecutor, had taken a class action against Belpietro, claiming that 'the term "Islamic bastards" is a general insult to one and a half billion Muslims, many of whom are victims of terrorist attacks'. In court, Belpietro defended himself by claiming that he 'assumed' that the insult 'referred to terrorists, because *'Islamici'* was the adjective relating to the noun *'Bastardi'* and served to define the Islamic matrix of the attacks', so his sentence was not intended to insult Muslims.

The judge found in favour of this line of defence and declared *'il fatto non sussiste'* – that there was 'no case to answer'. But there is a case to answer: there is continuous demonization of Islam, and such articles are part of it.

On the pretext of free speech, the media spread and foment hatred of Islam. Decent, intelligent, and politically correct language that respects the sensibilities of others has been thrown to the winds. In the language of the media and the politicians, bullying is increasing at an unprecedented rate towards all Muslims, including Italian citizens of Muslim faith. On the pretext that the 'Judaeo-Christian roots' of Italian culture must be protected, it is suggested that a culture can develop on its own and is not shaped through dialogue and collaboration, which denies the contribution that Arab-Islamic civilization made to the Renaissance and the Enlightenment in Europe. On the pretext that links Islam to terrorism, people are forced to pray in garages and basements, not to mention on pavements: they are denied the right to open a mosque. In real life, terrorism kills Muslims every day, but in the eyes of many these lives do not count. Instead, the so-called 'Islamic countries' sign contracts amounting to billions of dollars and euros to buy arms from Western governments.

It seems to me that many of my countrymen are uninformed and are being manipulated. On talk shows politicians and journalists discuss Islam without any specific preparation and fill their mouths with terms such as 'Jihad' – understood only as an instrument of terror, or 'Sharia' – a legal subject so vast that it requires years of university study. I ask for nothing more than my rights as an Italian Muslim citizen to be respected. I ask for a little reciprocity.

Italy for me is my step-mother, but can I be sure she accepts me?

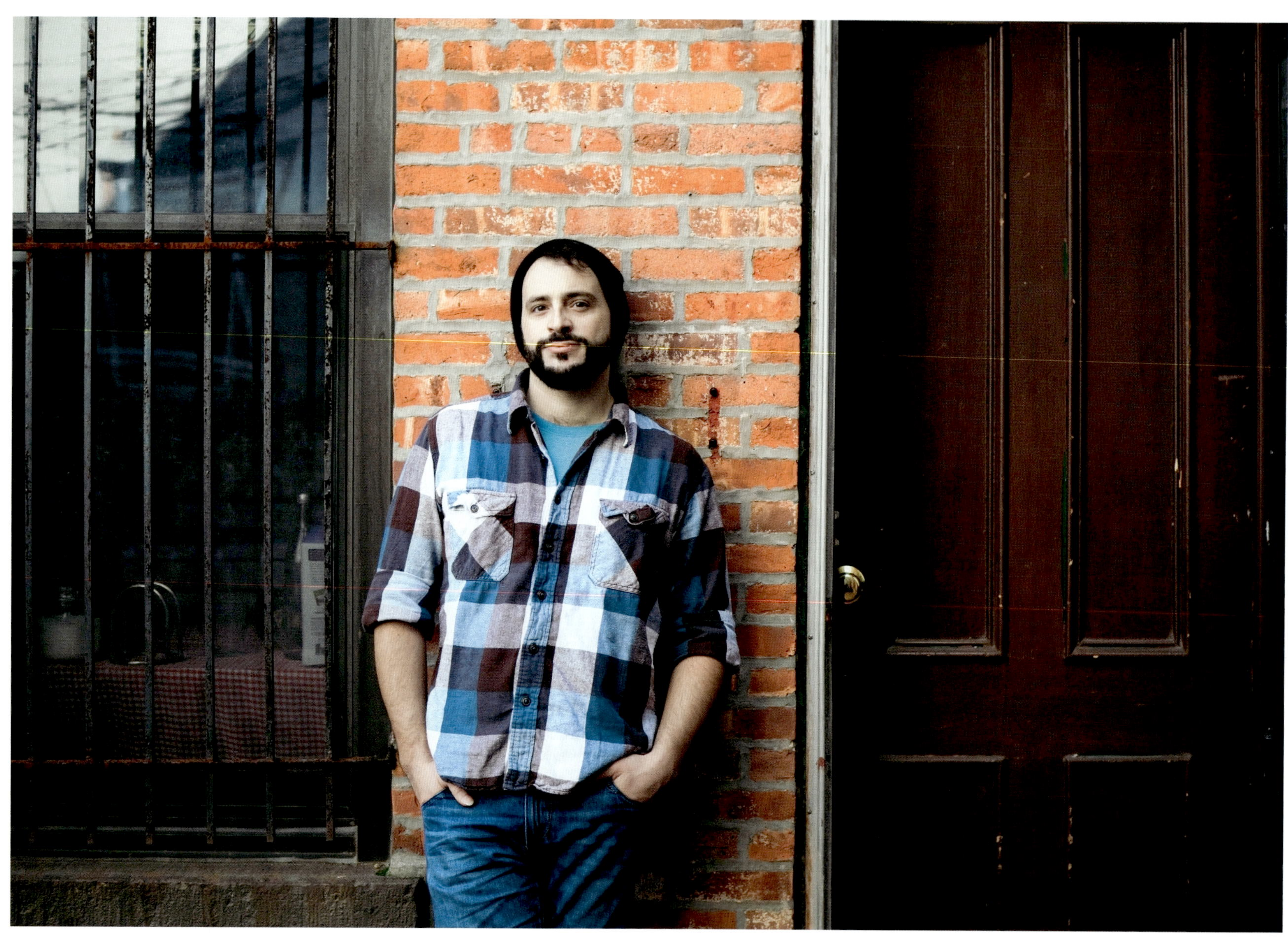

Francesco Guercio, a musician and researcher, grew up in Rome and has a degree in Philosophy. He moved to America, and subsequently got married. He now works and lives with his wife Rebecca in New York. Brooklyn, New York (USA) 2016.

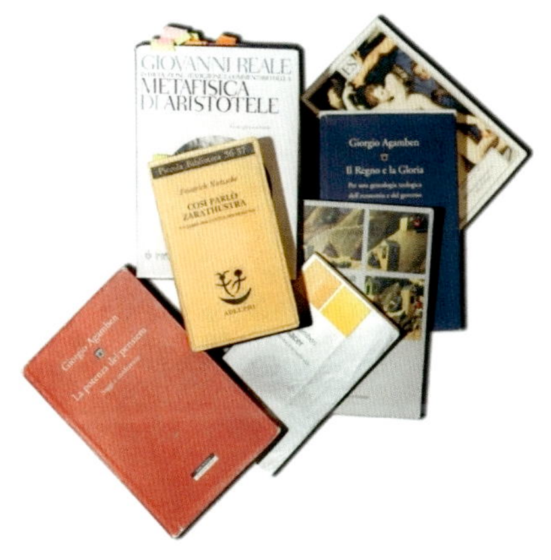

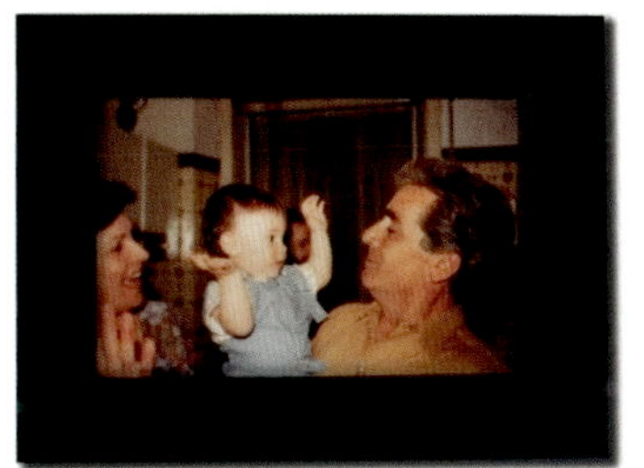

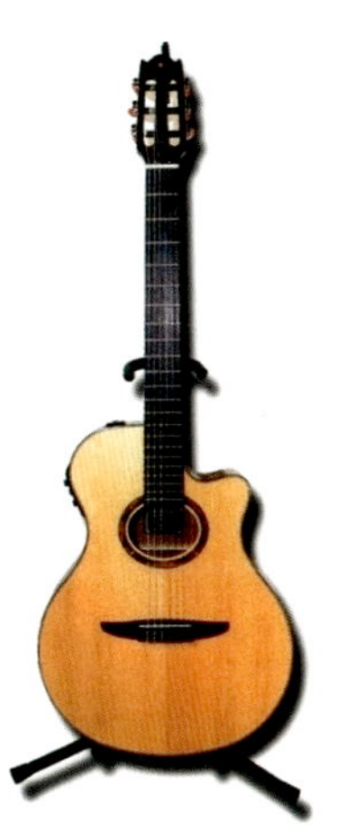

1. Francesco's philosophy books; 2. A photo of Francesco with his maternal grandparents; 3. His inseparable guitar brought with him from Italy.

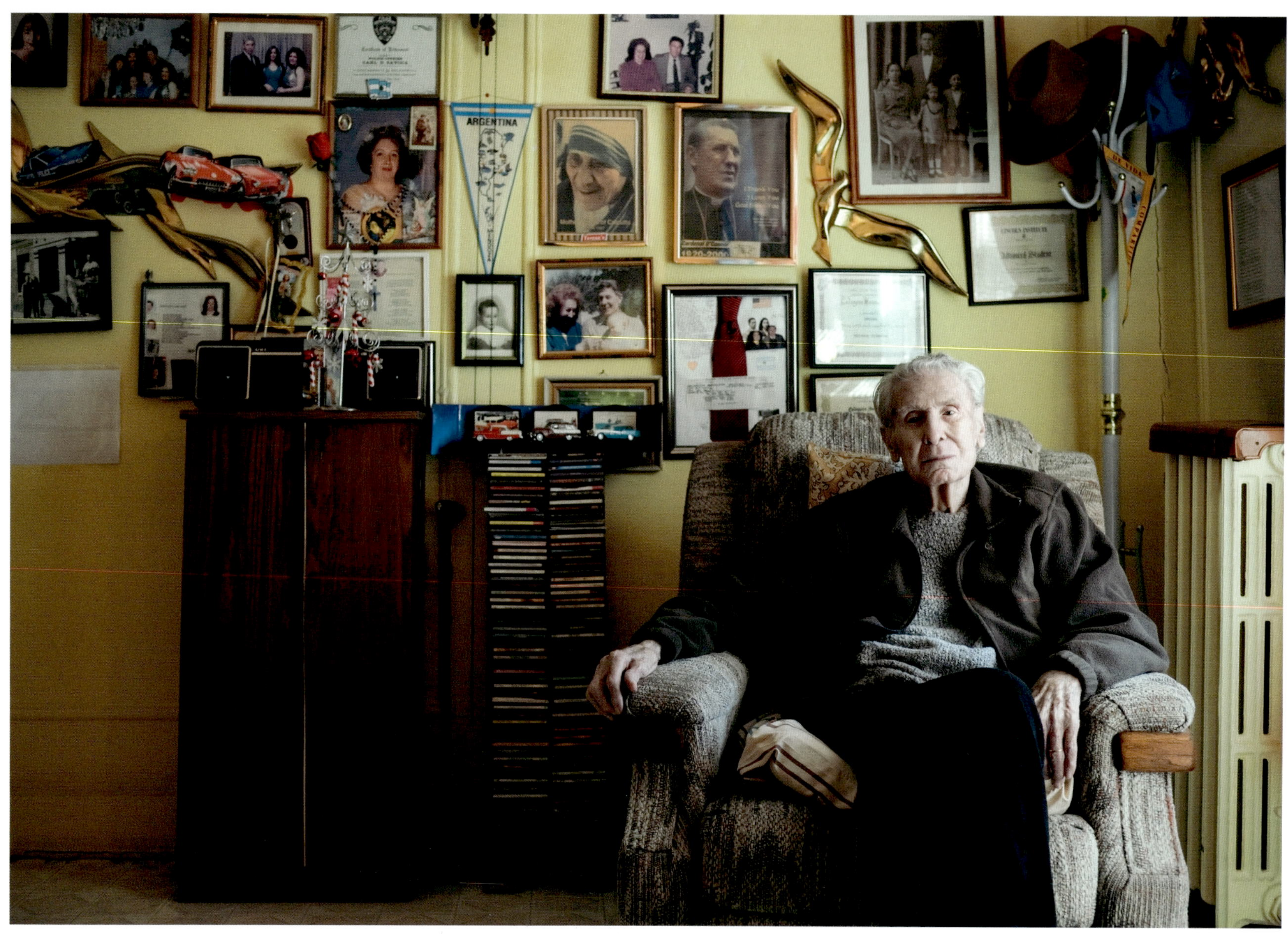

Calogero Savoca's family originally came from a village near Catania in Sicily. When he was only ten days old, his parents set off to Argentina and Calogero's first months were spent on board the ship. His father had been a policeman, but once they settled in Mendoza, he opened a very successful pasta shop. Calogero joined the police force in Argentina and ended up mediating between soldiers and security forces during the coup against Perón. His daughter remembers the family with their ears glued to the radio waiting for news. The family moved to New York in 1959 and Calogero went back to visit his family in Sicily for the first time when he was 78. His favourite place is still Argentina. Bronx, New York (USA) 2016.

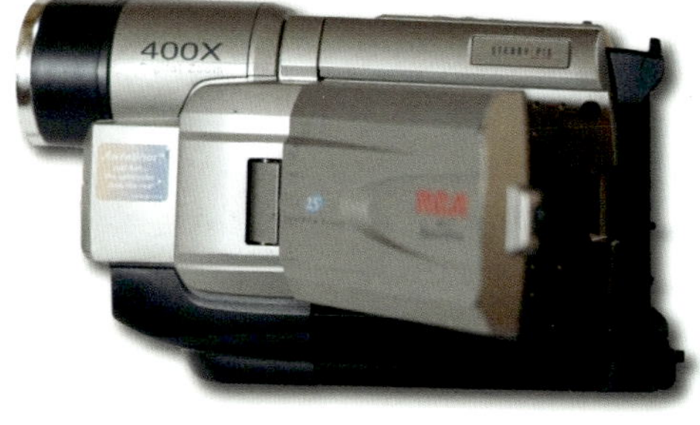

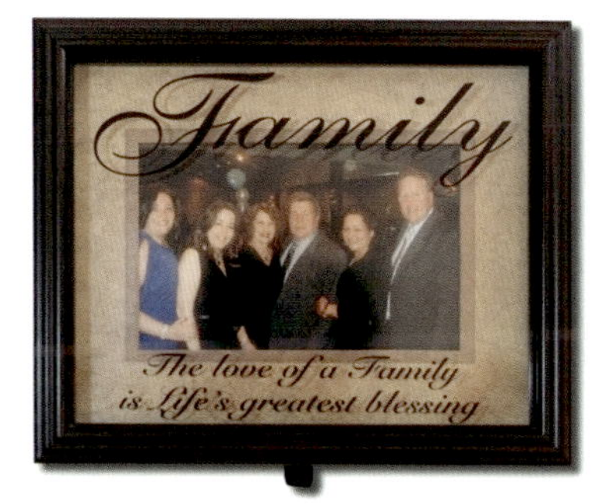

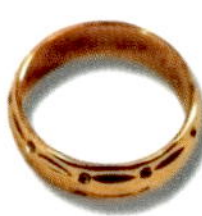

1. Calogero has always taken this camera on his many trips; 2. Picture of his daughter Marta and her family; 3. The wedding ring of Maria Elvira, Calogero's wife who died some years ago.

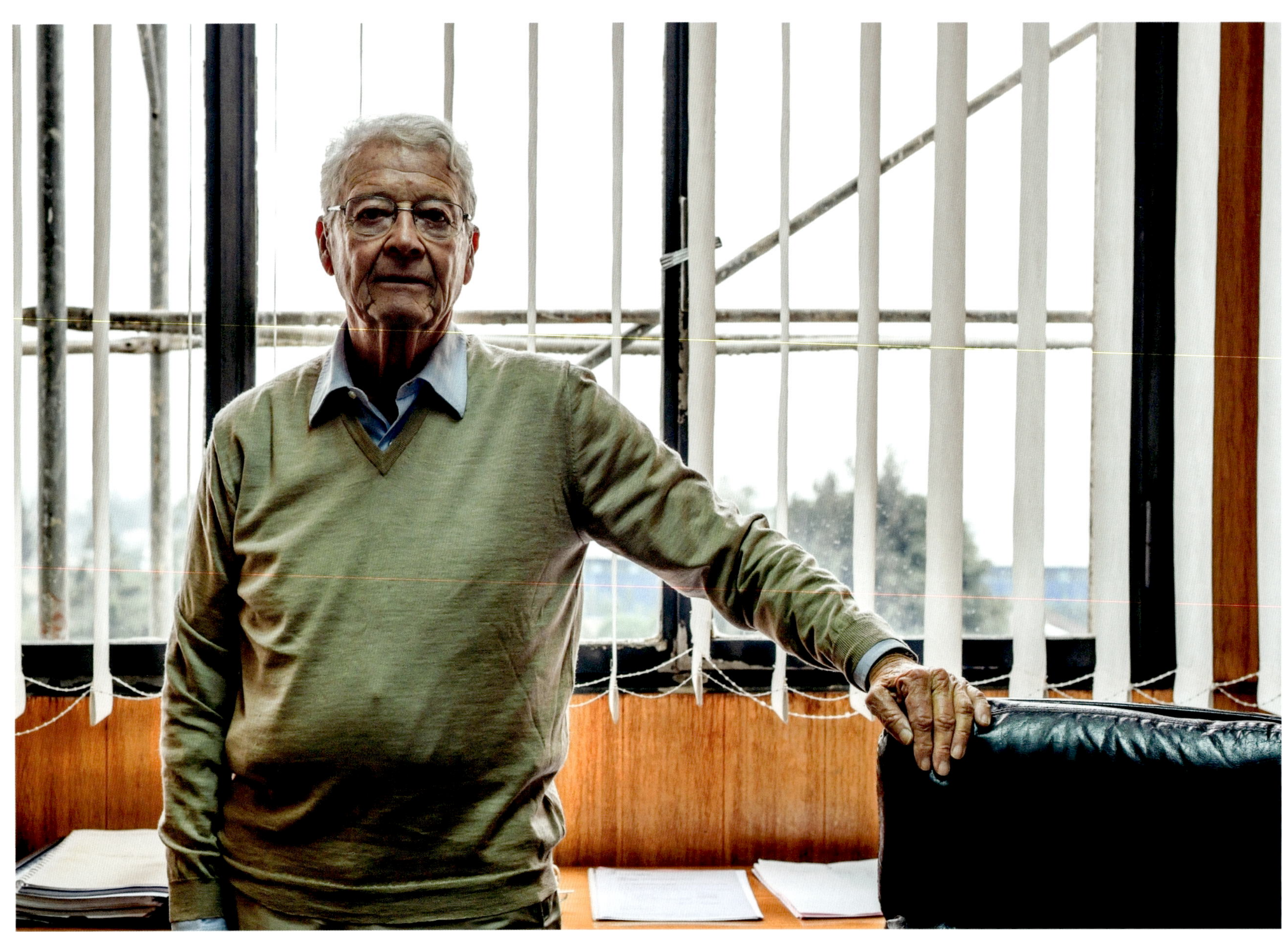

Alberto Varnero was born into a family involved in the construction industry. His uncle moved to Ethiopia in 1910, followed by his father ten years later, where they started up a real estate venture. Alberto was born in Asmara in 1942, and after graduating at the Politecnico Engineering school of Milan he returned to East Africa to take over the family business. The company is still thriving today, under the leadership of Alberto's son. Addis Ababa (Ethiopia) 2017.

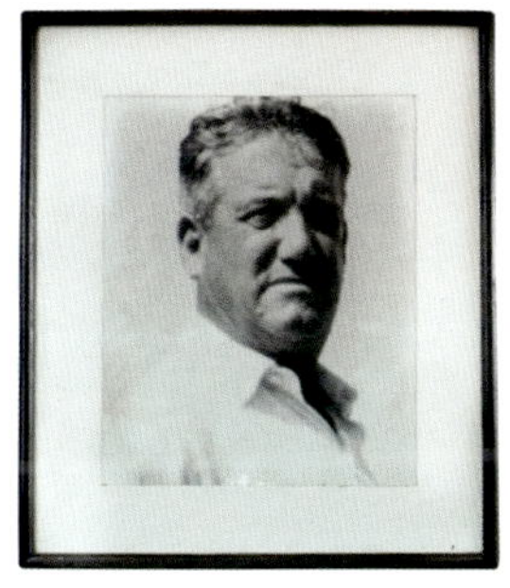

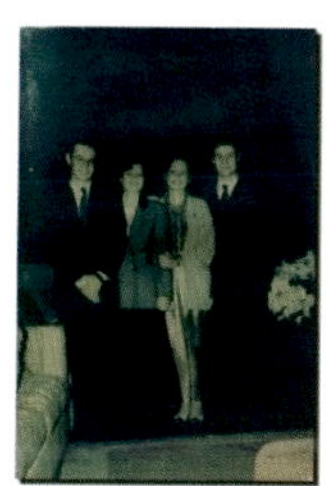

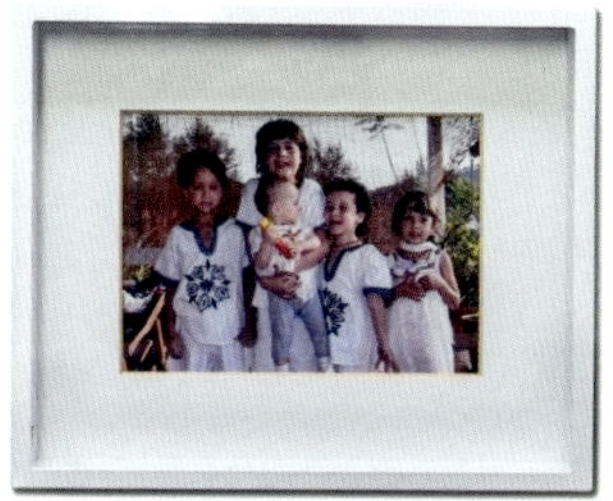

Alberto Varnero selected three photographs representing three generations of his family. 1. Alberto's father; 2. Alberto's children with their wives; 3. Alberto's grandchildren.

ITALIAN MIGRATION/ PERSONAL EFFECTS

Georgia Wall

She was from the part of the country that had been at the very edge of the Kingdom of the Two Sicilies. Bordered by the Adriatic Sea to the east and the Apennine mountain range to the west, this area has always been remote. The earth bears the imprint of the *transumanza*, the practice of driving sheep from the cold highlands to the warmer coastal plains for the winter and back again the following spring. The wide paths carved out by centuries of this twice-yearly migration are an enduring geographical feature. Her brother-in-law had been a shepherd, his feet one of the thousand pairs that had shaped the landscape. I was shocked to find that, when he visited, he curled up on her cold tiled floor at night to rest; after a lifetime as a transhumant pastoralist, he was unable to sleep in a bed.

The writer Natalia Ginzburg, in one of the few literary portraits of the region, highlights the isolation and stillness of its vast and silent countryside, describing the time she spent there as 'exile'. 'Our city was far away, and far away were the books, friends and variable events of a real life', she writes in *Le piccole virtù*, implicitly contrasting her 'real life' with the monotony of that of the ruddy-faced women she observes huddled into their black shawls, walking to church in the snow. I wanted to include this anecdote in the class I had to prepare on this author, to dispute the flatness of that image, to conjure for my students the openness and worldliness of one of those wrapped-up faces and map out the threads connecting her to the world that Ginzburg thought so distant.

Because I moved away not too long after she died, it is easy for me to picture her there still – seated alone at the table, eating bread pobs or playing solitaire or staring quietly into the distance, occasionally smoothing down the tablecloth. Her literal immobility (she only left her apartment once, as far as I am aware, in the last ten years of her life, to celebrate her granddaughter's university degree at a small restaurant nearby), the quality of her stillness the focal point in a room brimming with the materiality of mobility.

When I told her where I was from, she told me with a wry smile that her husband had warned her never to trust the English. He had been taken prisoner by English soldiers. He had ended up in Australia, well-loved by a farming family who had begged him to stay, she said. They had even promised to leave him their own land – think about that. But he had come back to Italy and to her – just walked through the door, as if he were returning from a day's work. She showed me the essential vocabulary booklet he had been given as a prisoner of war, which she kept in a little tin on the dresser, next to a set of shot glasses her granddaughter had brought back from Ireland. At the top of the second yellowed page of Gill Sans print, more useful text had been added by hand: 'ded', 'aim sori'.

She had moved to the seaside town before it changed its name and became the provincial capital, before two towns were merged and grew into a bustling port city, but she kept the mountain ways of her childhood and the stories she told were about life in a small hilltop town marked by mass emigration. *Compaesani* had gone to 'la Mèreca'; to New Jersey and Canada, Belgium, and Germany. She remembers walking to school and eating cherries in the snow. That's why she cooks bean broths in August, her daughter added, fanning herself in the torrid heat as I consider the suggestive and improbable combination of snowflakes and cherry blossom; that's why, when my brother had something to say about it, she clouted him with that ladle. At this, the old woman feigned brandishing the ladle and they both laughed. Her cooking utensils are all worn and smaller than modern ones. There is one large pan lid, dented through years of use and with a handle made out of half of a wine cork, a repair which bespeaks her unassuming ingenuity.

I find her in unexpected places. The beat of a synth-pop song transports me to another afternoon round her table: the screenwriter of *La Dolce Vita* came from these parts, her daughter is telling me, and *paparazze*, the local word for clams, provided the inspiration for the name of the film's intrusive photographer. She mimics the mechanical clicking of camera shutter leaves, while miming with her hands the opening and closing of shells. 'Really?', I turn to the old woman, fascinated. 'Who knows?' she shrugs and smiles with her typical abstract interest. A student's social media post – a filtered image of an Italian herbal liqueur with the tagline 'my dad's hangover cure' – is an uncanny echo of her own description of the properties of the same drink, which she offered guests after coffee. Coffee. Her aluminium moka pot. She cooked for one, but there was always someone round for coffee. Her remaining siblings, cousins, her children and grandchildren, students renting the apartment opposite; they all called in for coffee and often brought their own guests. She added sugar to the pot directly and served the treacly mixture scalding hot in chubby ceramic white cups, sometimes on a tray. Her habit of sitting in silence as it brewed on the stove coaxed a story out of the most taciturn guests, so it seemed that the moka pot itself was listening, its beaky spout expectant. After her death, her sister took the pot and, when she too died, it passed to her granddaughter.

ITALIAN MOBILITIES:
A View from Tunis

Barbara Spadaro

I had the opportunity to explore with Mario Badagliacca many forms of Italianness as we travelled across the research contexts of a pioneering academic project on the global dimension of Italian culture. The journey proceeded through transnational and local networks, intertwining on the paths of our respective researches in Scotland, Rome, London, Addis Ababa, Tunisia, and Liverpool, where we met for workshops, interviews, and exhibitions. Each meeting was an exchange of knowledge that shaped my understanding of the project and each exhibition provided a novel opportunity to engage not only with fellow members of the research team, but also with visitors who would eventually turn into participants for new strands of the project. This happened in Tunis, where I had many conversations with the local visitors to the *Italy is Out* exhibition at the Italian Cultural Institute. Many of the visitors were students and teachers of Italian, since – it emerges also in subsequent recorded interviews – the language in the country is still widely studied in schools and universities. We would talk about connecting with the stories, the objects, and the places in the photographs, while looking at the portraits of Italians from Ethiopia, Argentina, New Jersey, and Italy. Some students asked to borrow the exhibition concept, or an artwork for a school project. The portrait of Sara Tesfai for example – the student from Florence interviewed by Mario in Cambridge – was chosen by a group of undergraduates inspired by this representation of a successful Black Italian female student. Other visitors, rather than taking some photographs for their project, accepted to pose for Mario and engage in longer interviews, which started another series of journeys.

The interviews with Rita, Alfonso, and Vittorio illuminate the long and ongoing history of Italian mobility in the Mediterranean. This history of desire, travel, migration, and colonialism resonates within the processes of identifications of the participants of this project, between both interviewers and interviewees. Speaking Italian in multilingual Tunis is like diving into the fluidity of the Mediterranean and becoming part of it: 'Italian' in Tunisia is a current that draws deep memories to the surface, whirls around in wide circles, swallows up masses and particles, and eventually dissipates until the next tide. Participating in this project has been a constant exercise in self-positioning and identification with stories that resonate within the patterns, media, and languages of Italian memory in the Mediterranean – each with their own unique features and historical specificity, and each contributing to their resignification. Luisa Passerini would call this intersubjectivity, Alessandro Portelli, collaborative storytelling, as both concepts seek to illuminate the productive, relational nature of memory and subjectivity. By foregrounding the interdependency of language, memory, and subjectivity, our project explored this production as a form of translation. And in Tunis, Mario's invitation to translate stories through objects became an opportunity to explore some of the intricate trajectories of Italian memory in Tunisia.

The object that for me best represents these multidirectional trajectories, with their continuous comings and goings, is the wedding chest of Alfonso's great-grandmother. This wooden *cassettone*, made for her *corredo* (hope chest) in the mid-nineteenth century, travelled twice between Trapani and Tunis, with its imposing material and symbolic charge and with different generations of the family. The first time was in the 1860s, as part of the increasing wave of migration of Sicilians to Tunisia – a mass movement that the French protectorate wouldn't hesitate to stigmatize as infectious and illegal, and resisted with close monitoring and forced naturalizations, which Alfonso's family managed to avoid. Yet in 1960, after Tunisian independence, the family returned to Trapani, many of them continued the journey to the Americas, and nobody ever spoke about Tunisia again – at least, not in the presence of Alfonso. Decades later, as a young man pursuing his studies and academic career in France, Alfonso travelled to Tunisia from Paris rather than from Trapani like his forebears. While in Paris, despite all intellectual and sentimental affiliation, in his own words, he had always felt irredeemably *dépaysé*, in Tunisia he felt an immediate affinity with the colours, the sounds and the landscapes of North Africa, which changed all his plans. Alfonso ended up staying to research and write the history of Sicilians in Tunisia, including his own family's. His questions about his forebears' past in the country are still largely unanswered; though, who knows, some clues might someday emerge from a secret compartment in the *cassettone*, which Alfonso inherited and brought back to Tunis, as a familiar companion on his lifelong, half-real and half-imaginary journey of a Sicilian in Tunisia. A Sicilian who says that his 'returning home' is returning to Tunis (*'io "rientro" a Tunisi, per me il "rientro" è in Tunisia'*) as he finds home in the retracing and perpetuating of Mediterranean mobilities.

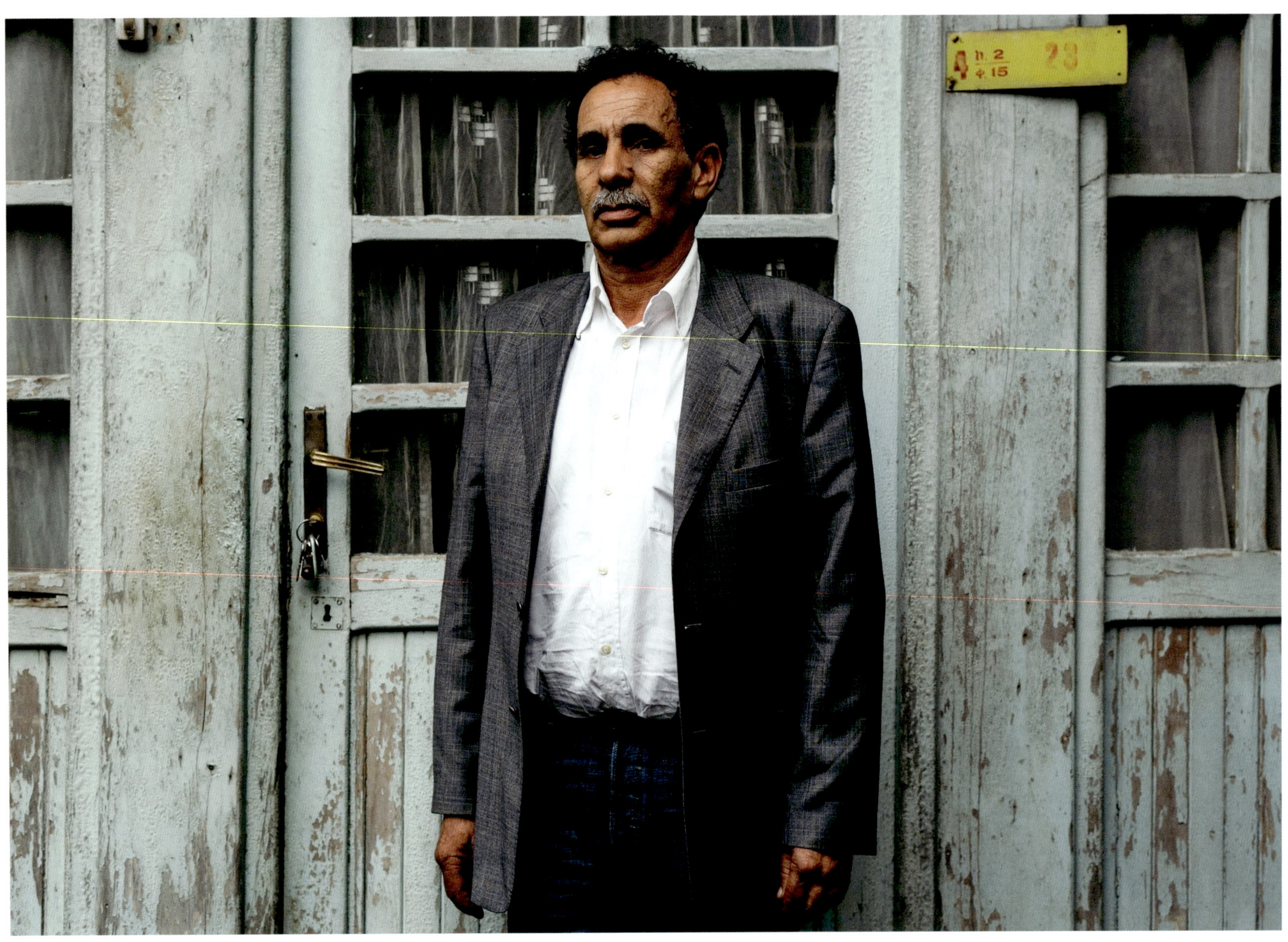

Alberto Di Lorenzo was born in Addis Ababa in 1954. When he was fourteen, Alberto moved to Asmara to study at the High School. After completing military service he stayed in Italy, working in the marble trade. In 1996 he returned to Addis Ababa to take up the running of the family carpentry business. Addis Ababa (Ethiopia) 2017.

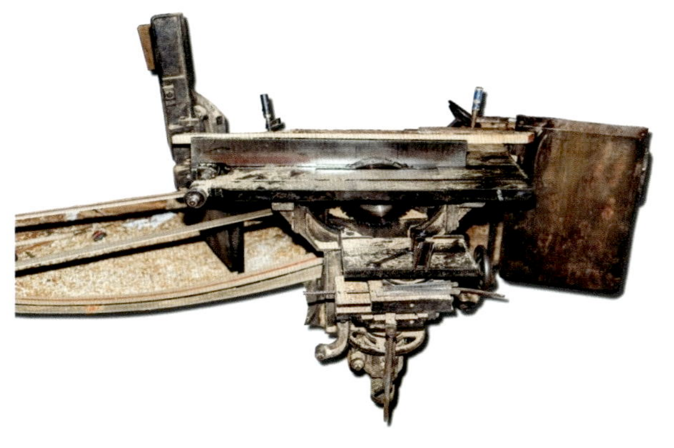

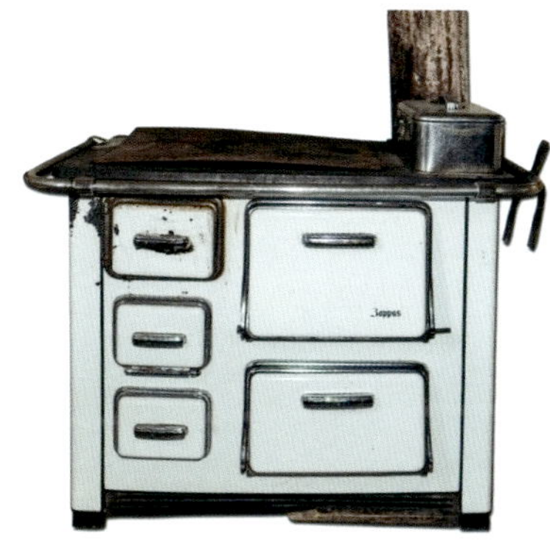

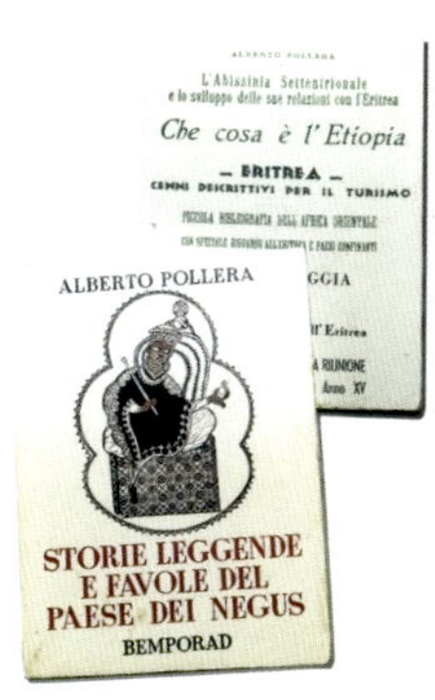

1. Carpenter's work bench; 2. Kitchen stove; 3. Ethnography books about Ethiopia written by Alberto's grandfather.

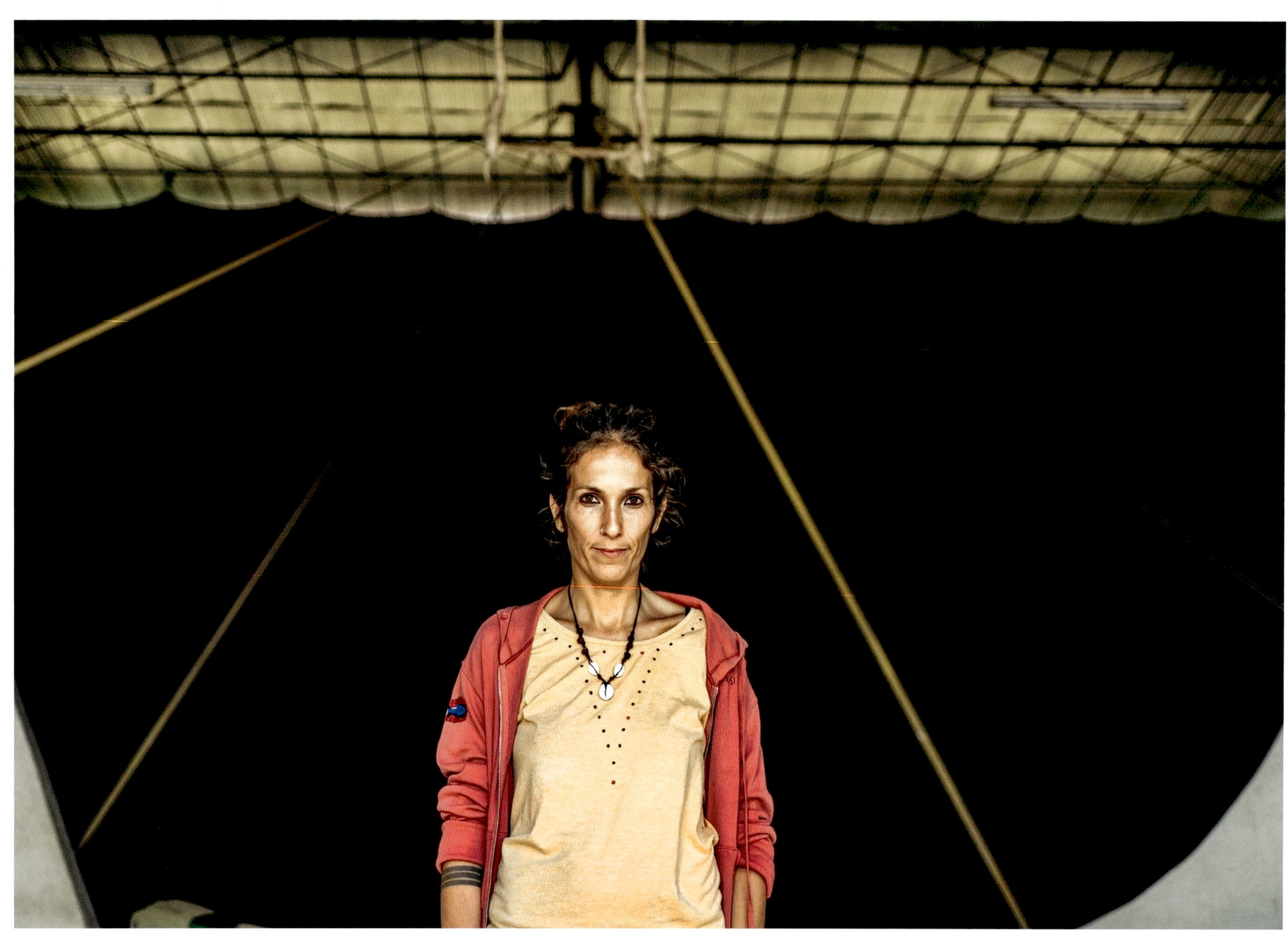

Giorgia Giunta has been living in Ethiopia since 2006 when she co-founded with her Ethiopian partner Fekat Circus (Blossoming Circus, in Amharic) a circus school and a social and cultural hub for young people in Addis Ababa. Over the last few years, Fekat Circus has been involved in international projects and toured extensively.
Addis Ababa (Ethiopia) 2017.

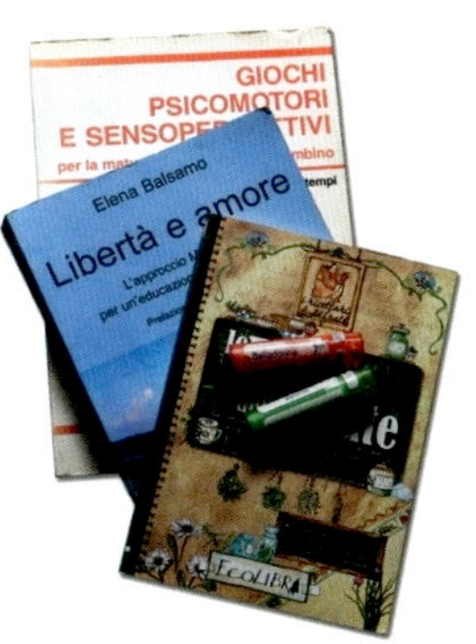

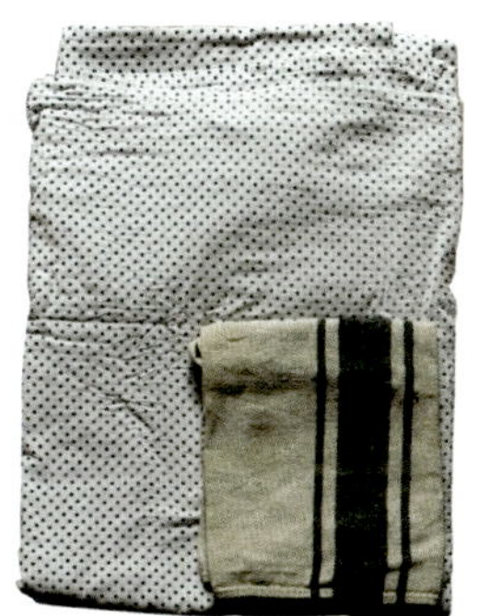

1. Pincers for developing and printing photographs used by Giorgia's father; 2. Education textbooks she brought with her from Italy; 3. Cotton sheets from/made in Italy.

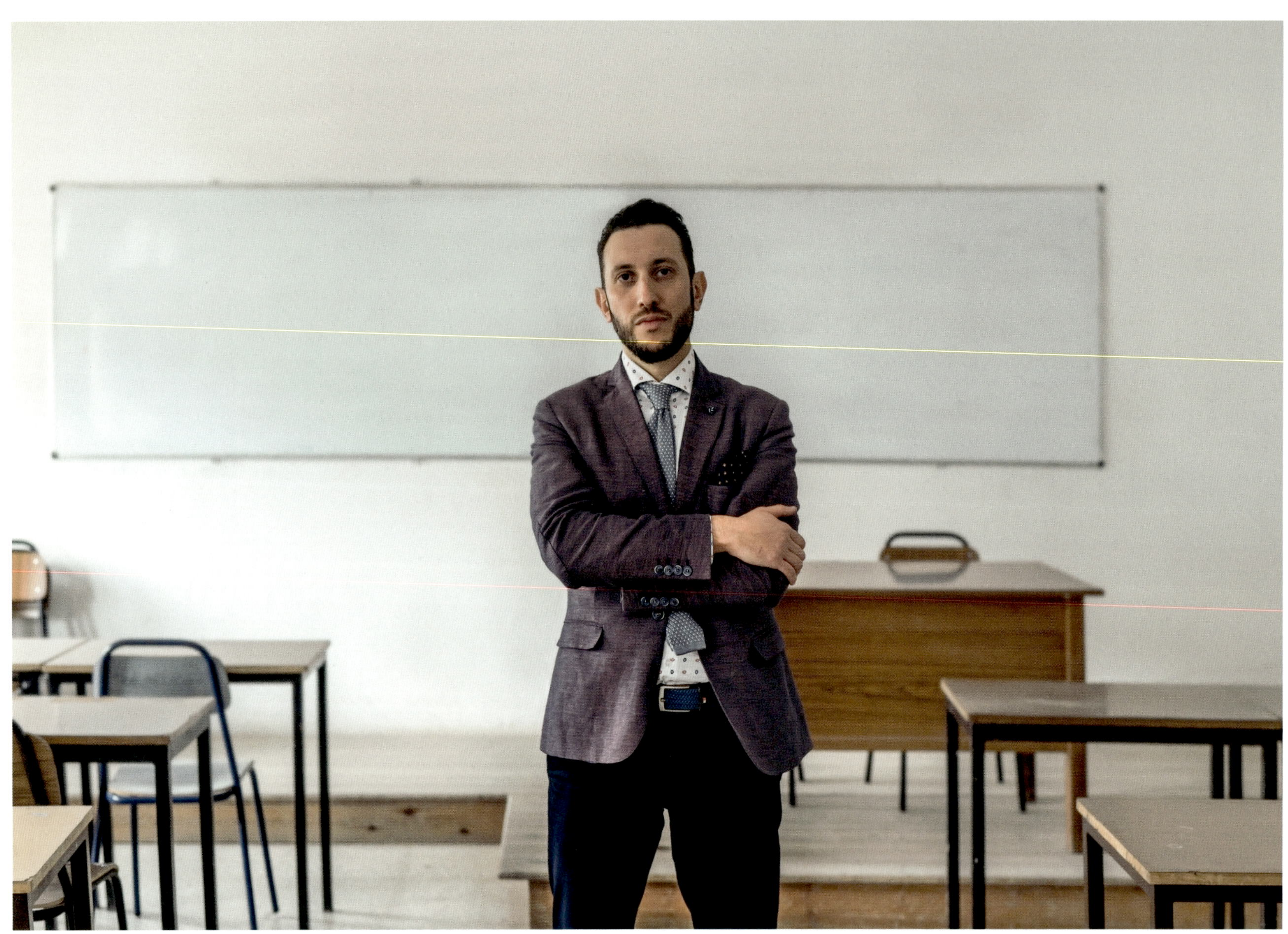

Vittorio Valentino from Pomigliano D'Arco (Naples). In the 1990s Valentino's father moved with his family to Toulouse after the aerospace company in which he worked decided to relocate staff. Valentino attended school in France and grew up in a multicultural environment, particularly with people from different parts of the Mediterranean. After some years teaching in France, he decided to move to Tunis, where he currently lives and teaches at Manouba University. Manouba (Tunisia) 2018.

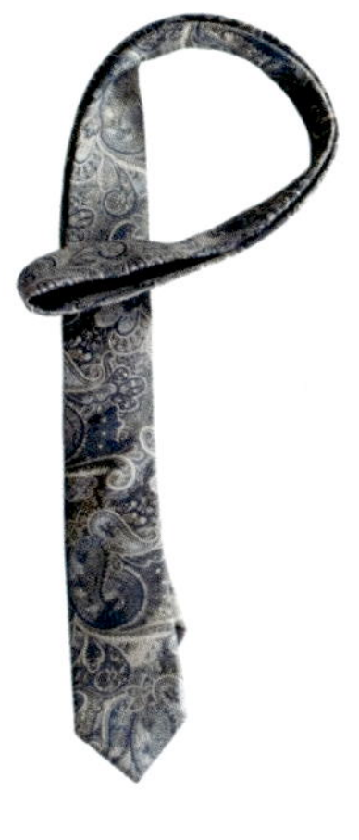

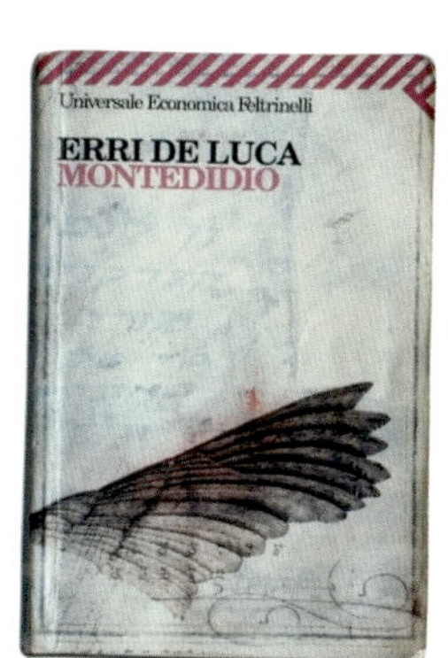

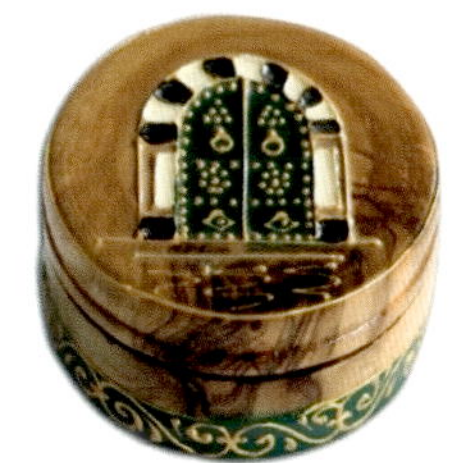

1. For Vittorio, dress is important. 'For me it should not necessarily be formal, but it's important not to be untidy'; 2. This book is really important for Vittorio; the writer Erri De Luca is from Naples, where Vittorio's family also comes from; 3. A Tunisian wooden box.

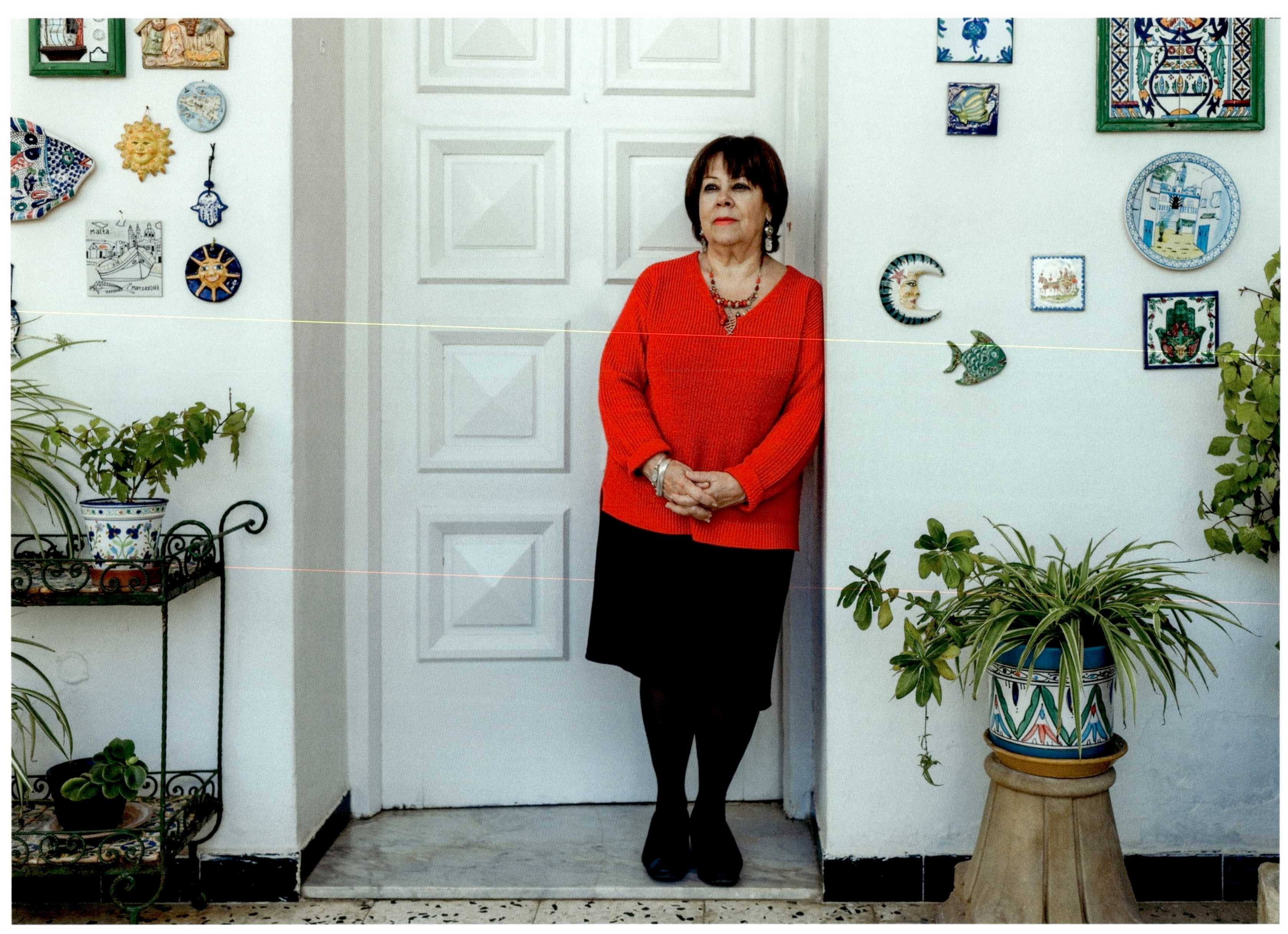

Rita Stazzera was born and grew up in Tunis but has Sicilian origins. Her grandfather was a fisherman and he moved from Marsala (Sicily) to work in Tunisia in the second half of the nineteenth century. His wife joined him there in 1907. Rita has strong memories of how racist the French authorities were towards Sicilians at the time of colonial occupation. Although Sicilians lived largely in their own community, they had close links with local Tunisians, and, especially after the Second World War, intermarriage became quite common. Tunis (Tunisia) 2018.

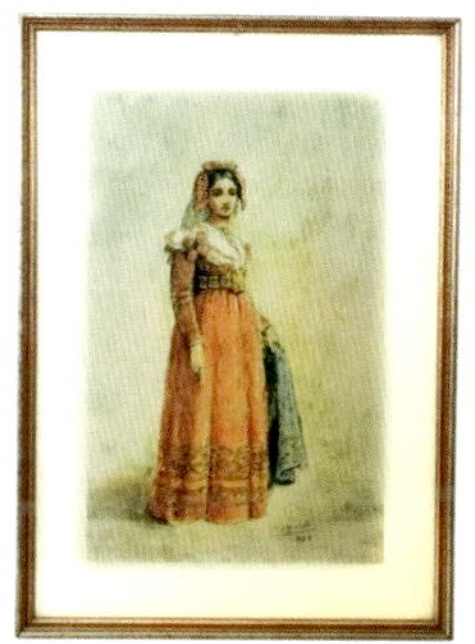

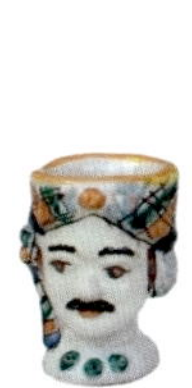

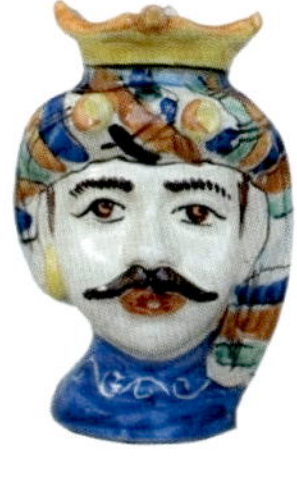

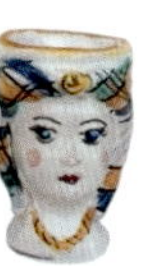

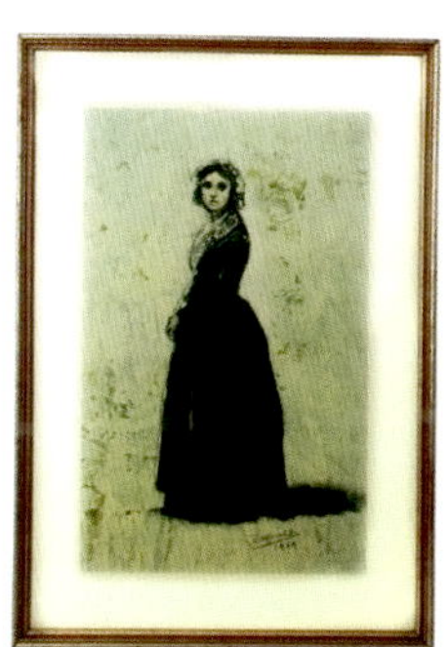

1. and 3. Paintings bought in Caltagirone (Sicily). Caltagirone is one of the most important places in Sicily for ceramics and artistic production; 2. The art of majolica pottery was brought to Sicily by the Arabs. Among the most important folk-art pieces are the 'Teste di Moro' (Moor's Heads), connected to an oral legend about a love story which took place around 1100, between a woman from Palermo and an Arab Man.

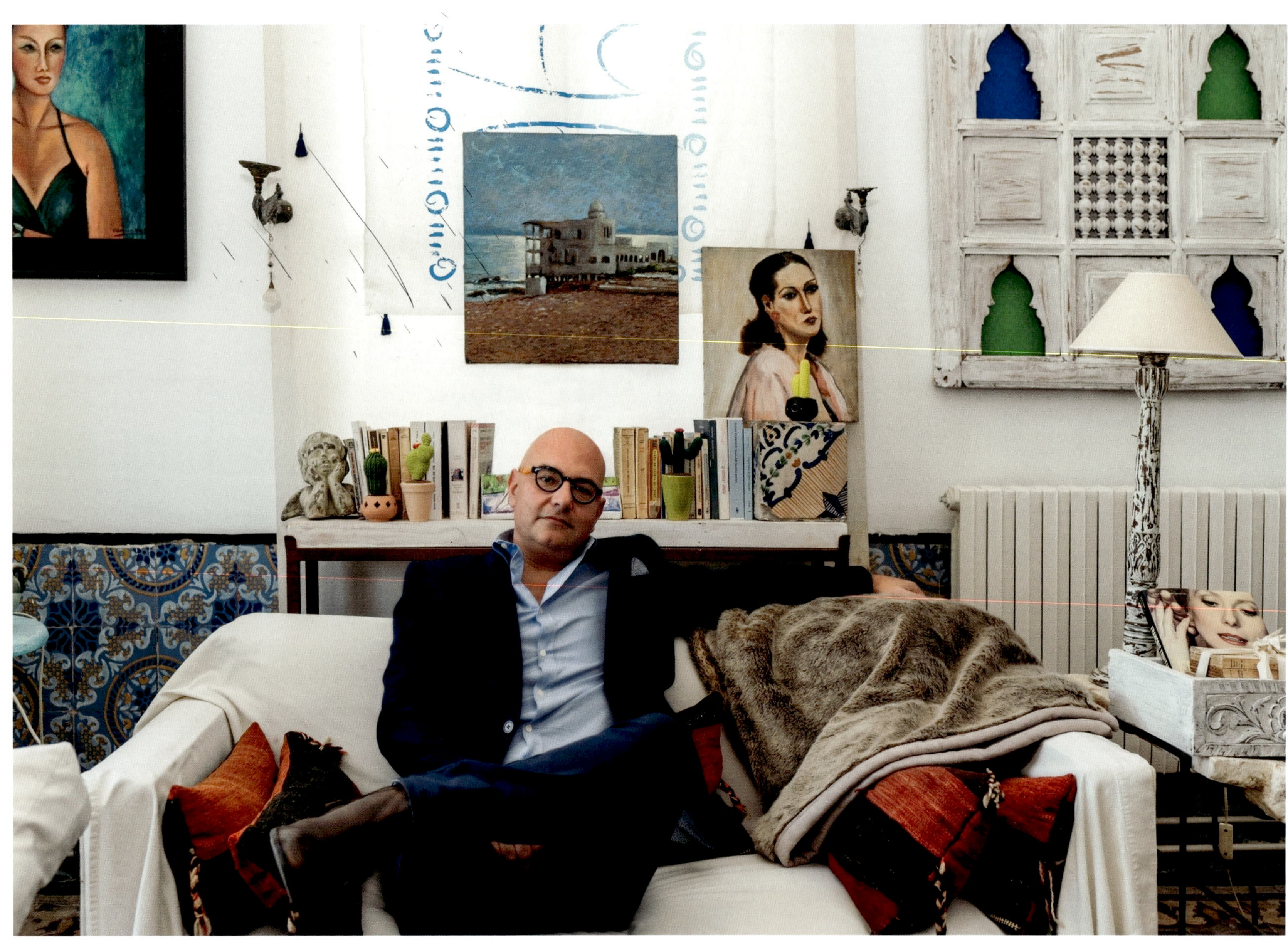

Alfonso Campisi is from Trapani (Sicily). After he graduated in Romance Philology and Italian, he obtained a PhD at the Sorbonne in Paris. The Sorbonne offered him a short-term position in Tunisia, but he then decided to stay there for a longer period of time and applied for Tunisian citizenship. Currently, he is a professor at Manouba Université, where he set up a course in Sicilian Culture and Language. He has written several books about the Arabic influence on Sicily and about the history of the Sicilian community in Tunisia. La Marsa (Tunisia) 2018.

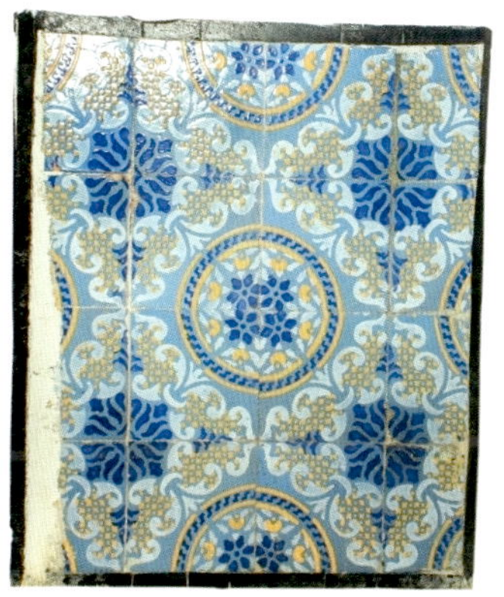

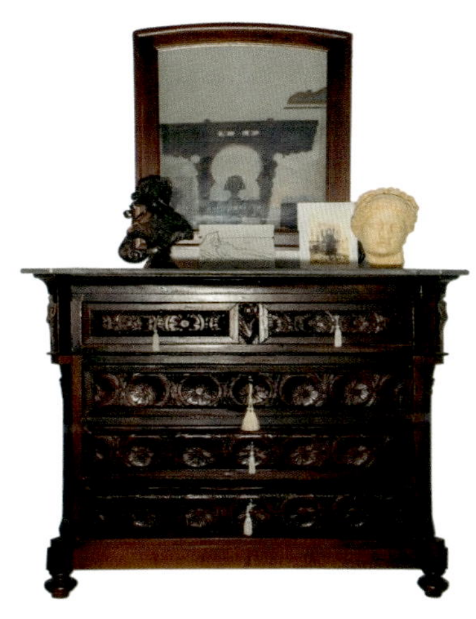

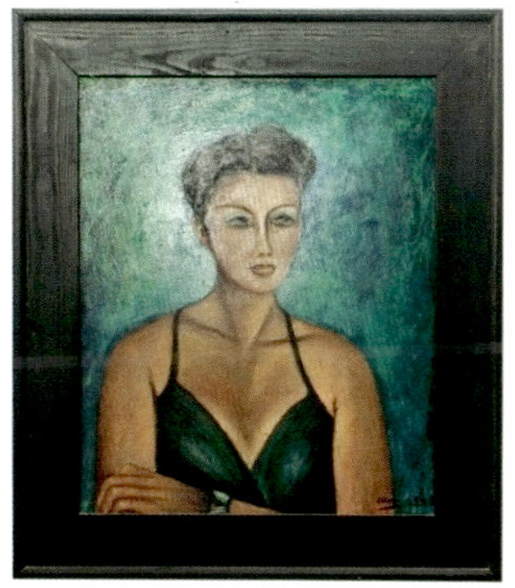

1. Majolica art was brought to Sicily by the Arabs. These wall tiles are used to decorate the houses of the Sicilian and Tunisian bourgeoisie; 2. Furniture made in 1861 that Alfonso inherited from his grandmother; 3. The painting represents Madame Baldanbembo, a Sicilian-Jew who lived in La Marsa. It was painted by Sauver Almenza, the last Sicilian member of the School of Tunis.

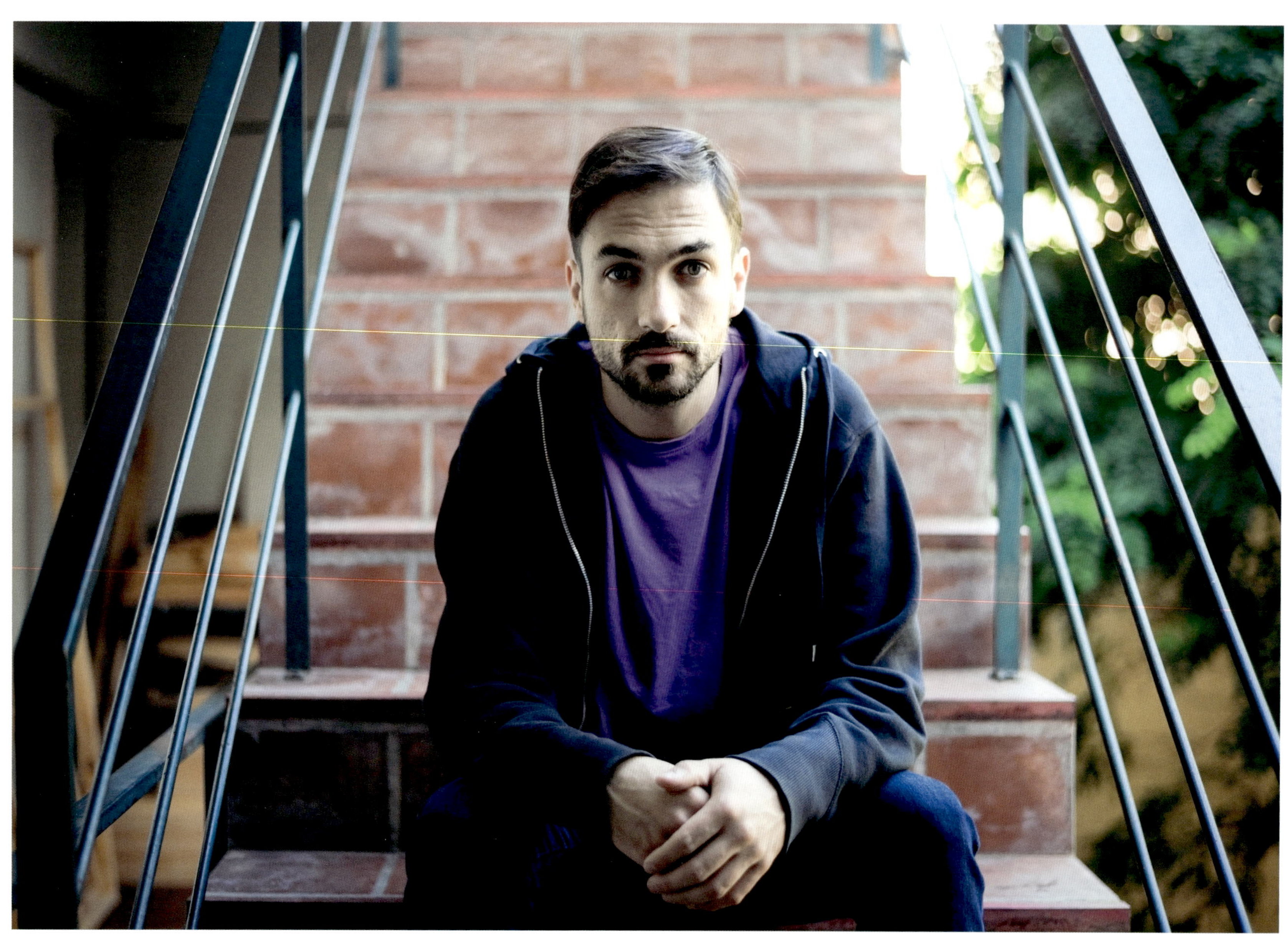

Riccardo Iorio graduated in Communication Science in Rome. In 2013 he moved to La Plata where he teaches Italian and has set up a new intercultural and artistic association, 'Espaguetti beat'. La Plata (Argentina) 2015.

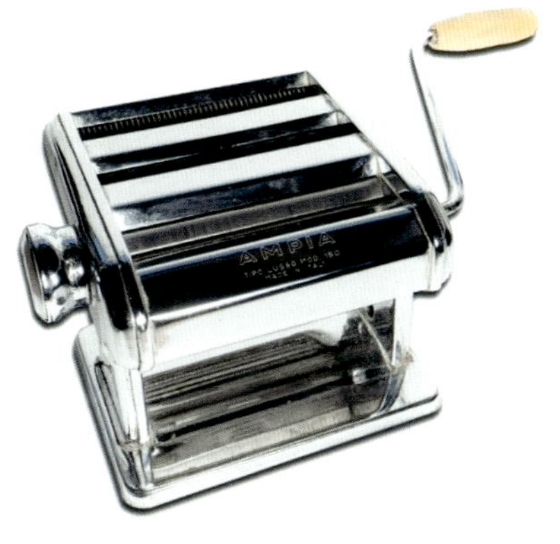

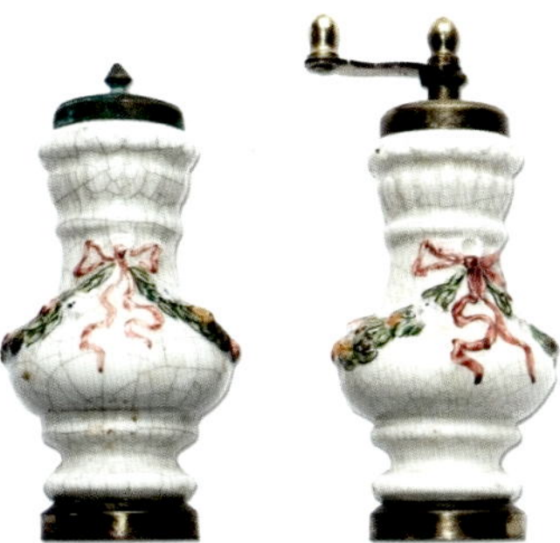

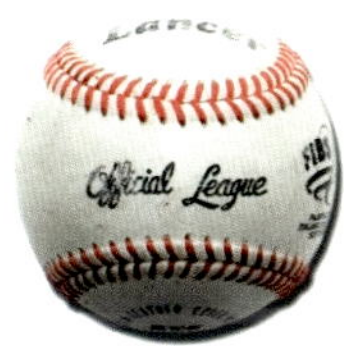

1. Pasta-making machine which Riccardo brought with him from Italy; 2. Riccardo's grandmother's salt and pepper grinders; 3. Riccardo grew up in Anzio, a coastal city south of Rome which has had a well-established baseball tradition since the sport was brought over at the time of the Allied landings in the Second World War.

FARE L'ITALIANO

Jacopo Colombini

The first time I saw the photos captured in Mario Badagliacca's *Italy is Out*, I was struck by how a quite diverse ensemble of people, backgrounds, and stories clustered around few recurrent *topoi* and objects in presenting and constructing transnational experiences of *Italianità*. The different temporalities and geographies represented by Badagliacca's subjects all appeared to summarize a sense of Italianness deeply characterized by nostalgia, a peculiar dependence on the identity-making value of food, and a sense of belonging to a 'homeland' that is not represented by an idea of Italy as a whole but, if anything, is captured by a constellation of regional and local identities.

Now, in writing these words in Germany, sitting at the desk looking at family photos and postcards from my home village in south Tuscany, I cannot help but wonder whether being or *fare l'italiano all'estero* is just a matter of feeling nostalgic, speaking Italian with some dialectal interferences, and making your homemade pasta. To a superficial eye, this might appear as a pretty harmless way to enact a national identity. However, cultural practices such as Badagliacca's work not only highlight how different forms of Italianness take place in the daily lives of many people that claim some sort of connection to Italy, but should also prompt a reflection on the cultural and political significance of reproducing national identities. For me, these questions have become ever more pressing with the birth of my first child, and ensuing questions around the cultural practices and competencies that I would like to pass on. Any form of nationalism, even minor and diasporic notions of Italy, enacts a sense of homeliness and belonging, but also reinforces its inevitably exclusionary manifestations in the homeland and beyond. Having dedicated first my academic and then professional career to trying to understand and fight xenophobia, racism, and the discrimination of people who decided to build a new life in Italy and Europe, the appeal of national identity is less enticing to me every day. Nevertheless, if anyone asks me who I am, I keep answering *sono italiano*. Why is it then so difficult, as Doris Sommer asks, to 'think and feel beyond' the national paradigm?

Despite living a transnational and mobile life, national identities still play a fundamental role in shaping our lives and access to fundamental rights. bell hooks has pointedly said that, in a world of passports, IDs, and visas, the 'burden of proof' of your nationality is unescapable. As researchers, artists, parents etc., we keep defining our disciplinary limits and ourselves through methodological nationalism, yet we still have the chance to refuse, oppose, and affect the only apparently monolithic boundaries and borders that we encounter in our lives. This can be achieved through forms of introspection that are not straightforward even for people in academia, sometimes too busy to study the 'other' rather than scrutinizing the self.

Badagliacca's work poses the question of what it means to be an Italian abroad today. Here instead, I want to shift the focus from the 'where we are from' to the *'how we think* where we are from'. Aligning myself with Stuart Hall, I argue that it's essential to think about our place in history as a social process and, at the same time, reflect on the tools we have to make sense of, or explain, our historical position. This means emphasizing the structural and conceptual constraints shaping our 'being' Italian, but also highlighting a certain degree of agency in the construction of our identities. If in Germany, Ireland, and Scotland, my Italianness was often projected on me by many people whom I met as a very frustrating mix of stereotypes relating to pasta, mafia, and jokes about Berlusconi, I have also learned how to use my 'being Italian' to counter these narratives and reshape their prejudice towards Italians or Italy in these places.

However, strategic essentialism or identity as a practice of positioning oneself against the hegemony of methodological nationalism and cultural stereotypes is not enough if we do not also attempt to offer an alternative to the racial and exclusionary underpinnings ingrained in the histories of national identities. The interstices in which these alternatives can take shape are not only to be found in what Donna Gabaccia defines as the more 'humble' everyday practices of the many Italian diasporas vividly captured by Badagliacca's photos, but also in the contexts and spaces that are not usually identified as Italian. Migrants and refugees (if we really need to use these categories) that come, briefly pass through, or decide to stay in Italy inspire and show us the possibility of embracing multiple identities, cultures, and languages without circumscribing them within the limits of the national, and use them as resources to find their freedom in a world of restrictions. During my research, I could not help but notice how in the everyday life of some members of the self-organized refugee group Lampedusa in Hamburg, the Italian language was not a primary source of (national) identification, but just another tool of communication in a fluid transnational and multilingual context. In this context, my mother language and my self-identification as Italian did not necessarily draw sharp boundaries of inclusion or exclusion, but sometimes created unexpected mutual understanding and, for brief moments, a sense of common belonging in a context of diversity and different privileges.

To conclude, in the many challenges posed by fatherhood, I never thought that of making of my son an Italian, *'fare l'italiano'*, would have been the one prompting more questions and self-reflection. Is it important that he feels Italian? If yes, what sort of *Italianità* do I want to offer him? Building on the experiences of the people I have encountered during my research, I would like to show him an example of Italianness that is not built on forms of *othering, rootedness* and, even worse, racialized differences, but on openness and proximity. Being Italian should be seen as just one of the many cultural competences and feelings that adds up to the ever-growing and ever-changing identities that make who we are in post-migrant society.

THE MULTIPLE LIVES OF THINGS

Margaret Hills de Zárate

Works of art serve to make our own experience and that of the world around us perceivable, an aim that resonates with the purpose of Mario Badagliacca's photographic essay, which invites the viewer to explore Italian migration through portraits and personal objects.

In almost all these portraits the subject is looking directly at the camera. The viewer meets their gaze as if they too were behind the lens, reminding us that these photographs are neither imitations nor interpretations of their subjects but rather traces of them at a certain place and moment in time. They belong to the subject in a certain purposeful way that serves to underline a sense of agency and intention, reiterated in the accompanying text, which is their account of Italian migration.

The frontality and directness of these portraits transmit a sense of familiarity that is reinforced by the setting, which is often a home. Moving from foreground to background, in the realm of the personal domain, are more images, as in the portrait of Calogero Savoca whose wall is populated with images of family. Unlike the subjects in the other portraits, he sits slightly further to one side of the image and, taking this as an invitation to approach, I catch myself leaning forward to be nearer, as if there in the room. In others we are close, as we might be in a conversation. We can see the detail of Elsa Gasparinetti's hands (the glint of her wedding ring) and those of Domenico Marraffini and Filomena Bolgona, their identical chairs pressed together, his hand on hers and his head inclined towards her. All, in one way or another, were caught up in the events that preceded the Second World War, its aftermath, or the volatile political situation in Argentina, and belong to a generation of Italians who were born in Italy and migrated to the Americas.

The children of the first generation of Italian migrants are represented by two women, Julia della Croce, whose father was from Sardinia, and Annalisa Pastore, whose parents were from Mola di Bari, in Puglia. They are portrayed in warm, comfortable settings, in seemingly established homes in the US. Particularly striking are the photographs of their fathers as young men, which point to travel and adventure, and the contrast between these objects and those that refer to domesticity and the home. There is a sheet embroidered by Annalisa's maternal grandmother, recognizable as an example of Italian women's needlework and one of the traditional means by which femininity was codified. The creation of *bianchieria* (white wear) involved the creation of towels, sheets, and so forth as part of a young woman's *corredo*, or trousseau, consisting of bed linens, tablecloths, and lingerie. The female members of the family would gather and hand-embroider fabrics as their contribution to the *corredo*, as would the girls themselves. Such objects, removed from their original context, retain a symbolic and cultural trace of a family's transgenerational identity.

Only one subject looks away, although all her chosen objects refer to her home in Florence and Tuscany.

Sara, as many of the other subjects of a younger generation of Italian migrants, is pictured in named locations but indeterminate places in which subjects are juxtaposed or set against backgrounds of doorways and windows. Sara seems to be looking far into the distance as she reflects on the nature of home and belonging and echoes my own thoughts about home which are of surprise by the many places that make her feel at home. England is one of these. Sara experiences herself as 'a balance of different cultures', an observation that is emphasized by the symmetry of the composition of the image itself.

Many of those who today are first-generation Italian migrants left Italy in the last twenty years, moving from one city to another. All have brought objects that signify their origins in Italy. Musical instruments, favourite books and, among these, a watch and a pipe that had once belonged to Riccardo Dessupoiu's grandfather.

That which at first seems static and ordinary becomes important because it has been singled out and imbued with something that is meaningful and significant. This pipe and the various objects that participants have chosen to share reveal much more than a simple one-to-one relationship. It is never simply this (object) standing in for that (thing) but points to something more, pictorially in their juxtaposition to other objects, or to their absence, and ultimately back to ourselves the viewer.

These photographs prompt us to reflect on our own relationship to belonging, to migration, and to its material traces. I see something of myself in Sara's averted gaze from the assemblage of my own family's portrait-chronicle of itself. In such collections, we may perceive or find evidence of ourselves, our connectedness, and a certain order. In mine this always seems to involve people standing in a particular order, with tall ones at the back and smaller members in the front line. Among these I find a trail of images of myself (from about the age of five), not looking at the camera but elsewhere at something outside the frame. And so the inevitable question arises as to what three objects would I take with me if I were to go elsewhere and where that elsewhere would be.

There are some places one cannot return to because, even if one could, the place has changed. Once I travelled from Lvov and took a boat from Alupka to Yalta in the Crimea to visit the White Dacha, where Chekhov lived and where he wrote a short story, 'The Lady with a Little Dog', of which Nabokov, another migrant observed, 'all the traditional rules of the genre have been broken … there is no problem, no climax, and ultimately no point at the end, yet it is one of the greatest stories ever written'.

I would choose the three chestnuts and a stone I took from Chekhov's garden.

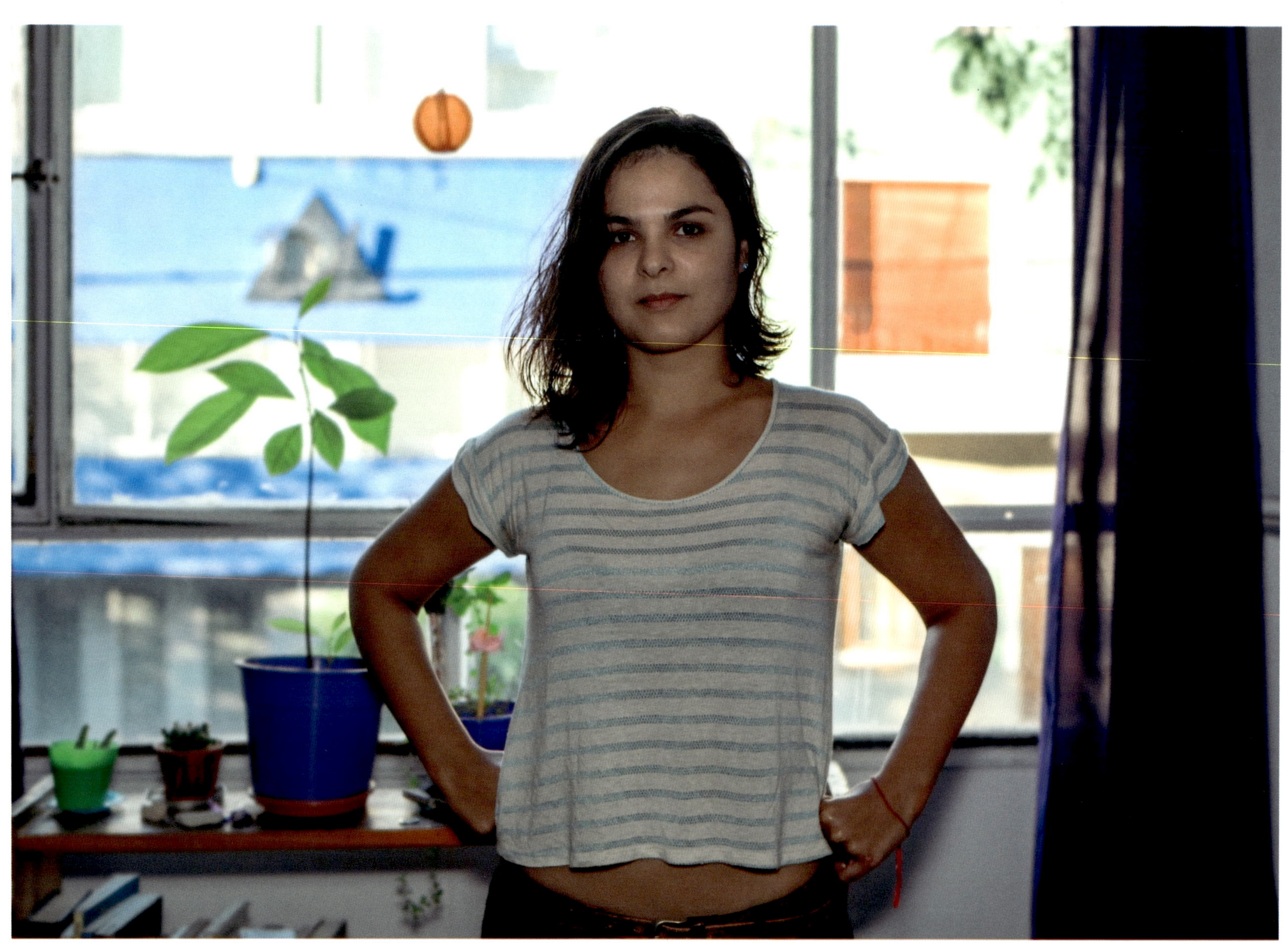

Andrea Cabrera grew up in San Martín de los Andes in the south of Argentina. Her great-grandfather Nicola Napolitano emigrated to Argentina from Potenza at the start of the twentieth century, and he was joined a few years later by the rest of the family. Andrea studied at the classical dance school of La Plata where she now lives and teaches contemporary dance and yoga. La Plata (Argentina) 2016.

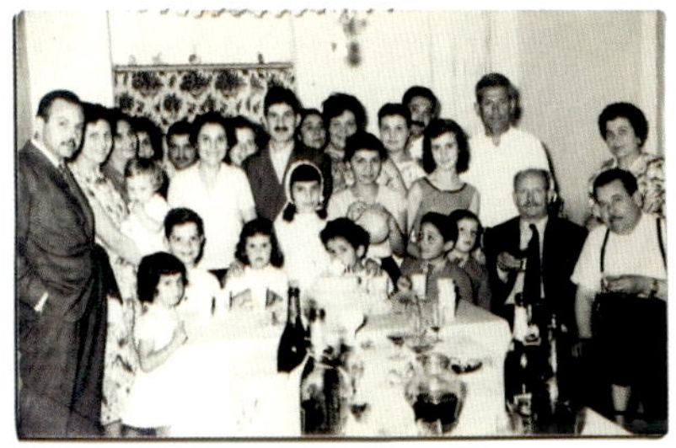

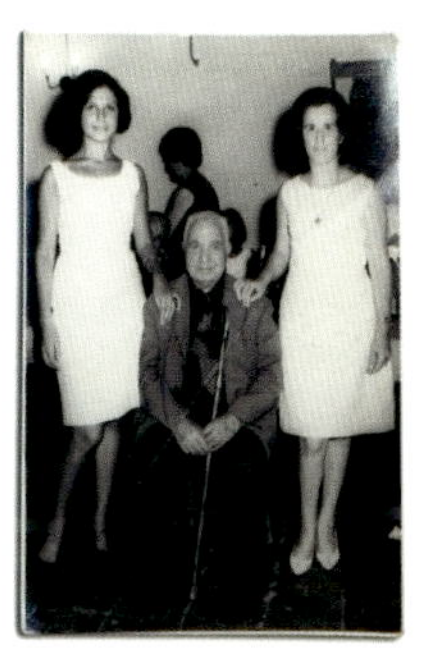

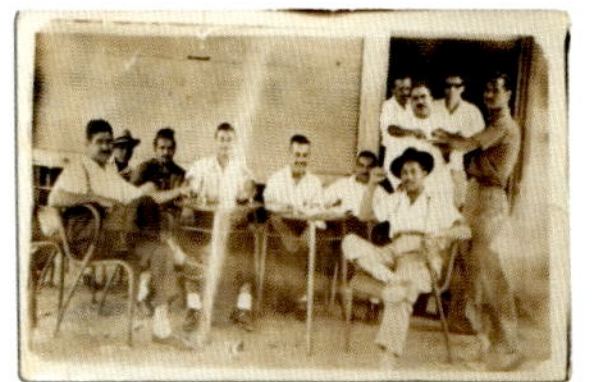

1. Family photo taken during Andrea's mother's communion; 2. Photo of her mother with her great-grandfather Nicola and cousin; 3. Photo of her grandfather, Vincenzo Napolitano, with other Italians in the second half of the twentieth century in Buenos Aires.

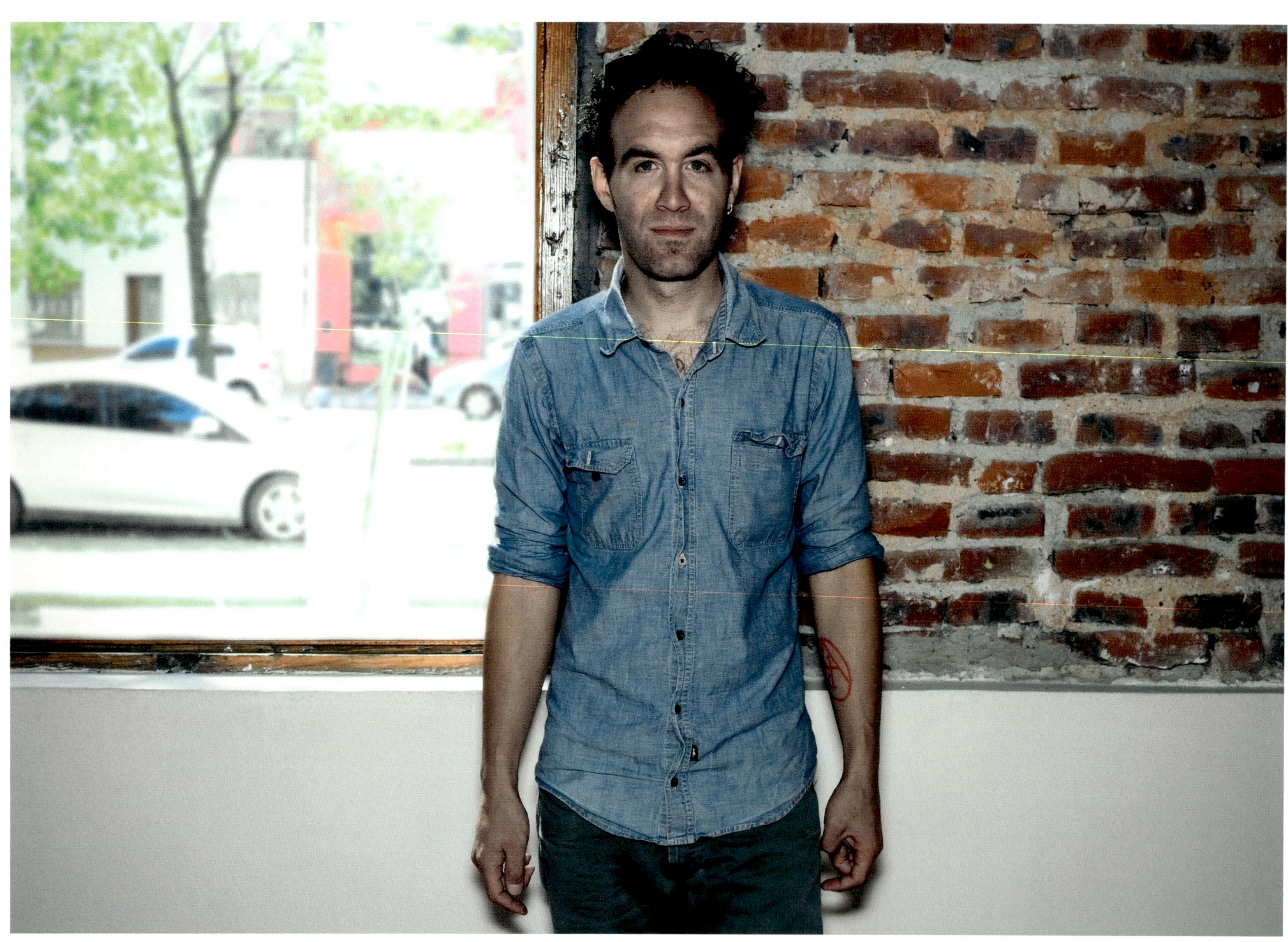

Riccardo Dessupoiu has Ligurian and Sardinian origins. He has lived in La Plata for eight years, where he married and where his son was born. At present he works in the culture sector and is a musician in various bands, playing a variety of genres from experimental rock to jazz. La Plata (Argentina) 2016.

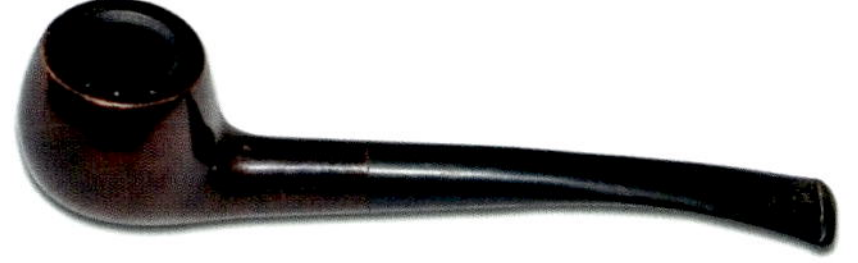

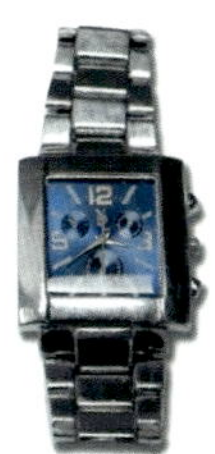

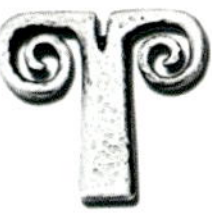

1. Riccardo's grandfather's pipe; 2. His grandfather's watch; 3. A rune which reminds Riccardo of Sardinia.

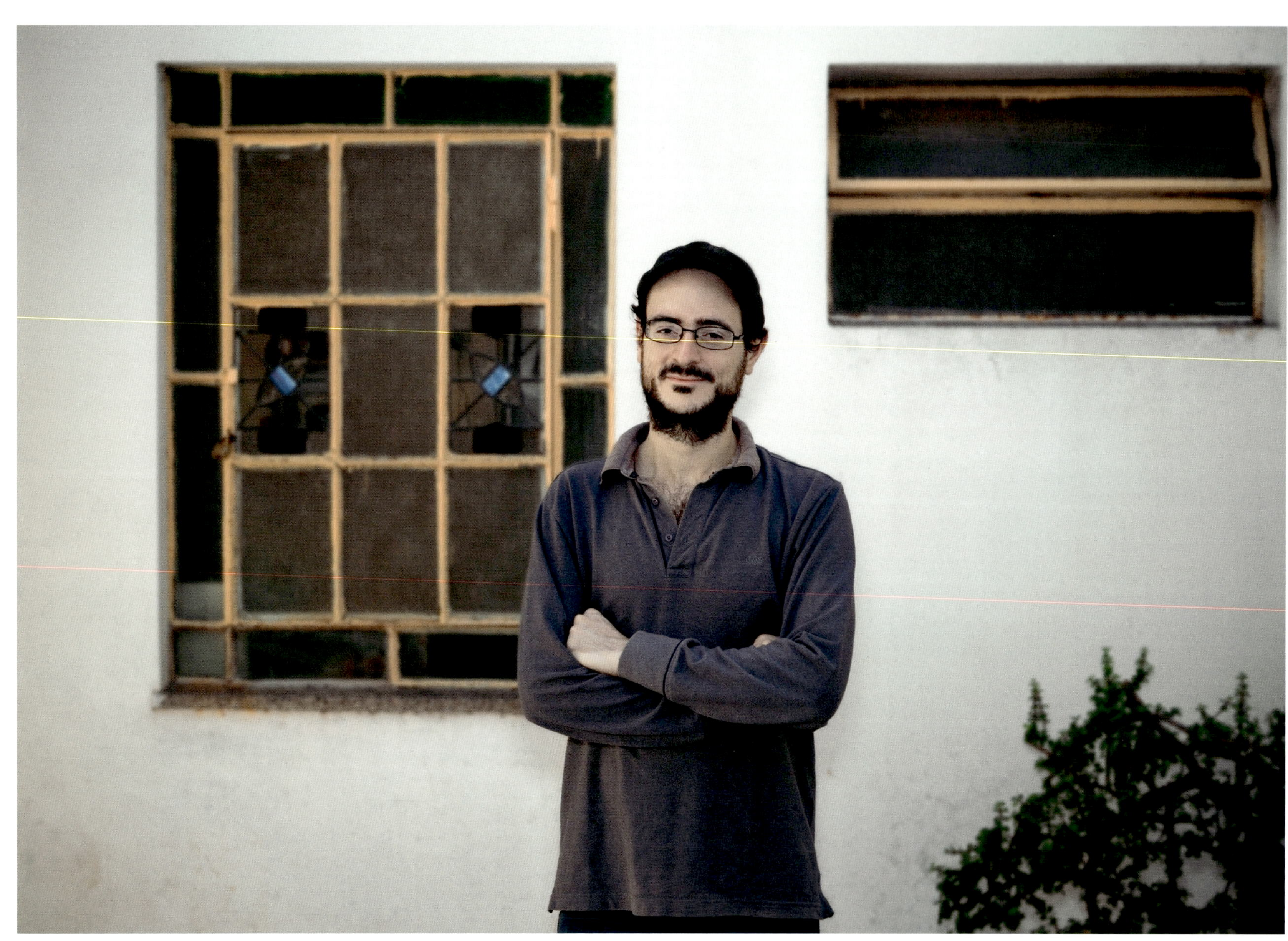

Simone Tolomeo is originally from Palermo. After a short stay in France, he decided to move to Argentina to follow his passion for music. Simone works with various music groups and plays and teaches the bandoneon. After living in La Plata for many years with his wife and daughter, he now lives in France. La Plata (Argentina) 2016.

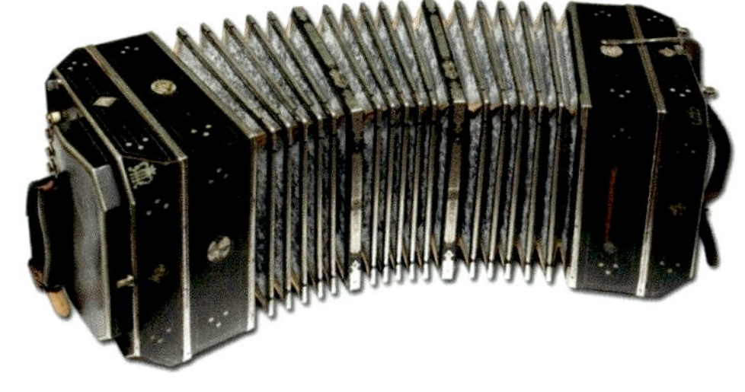

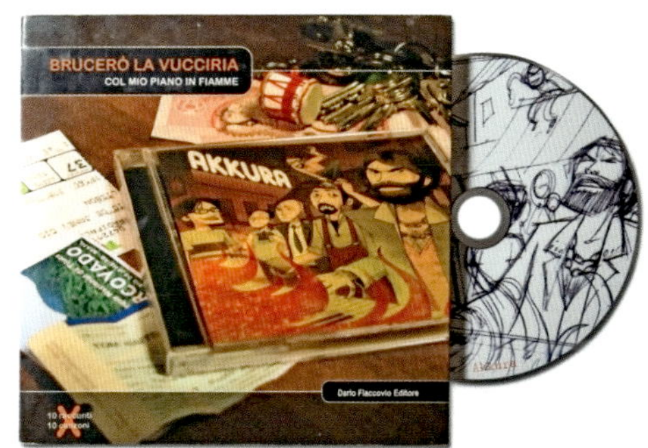

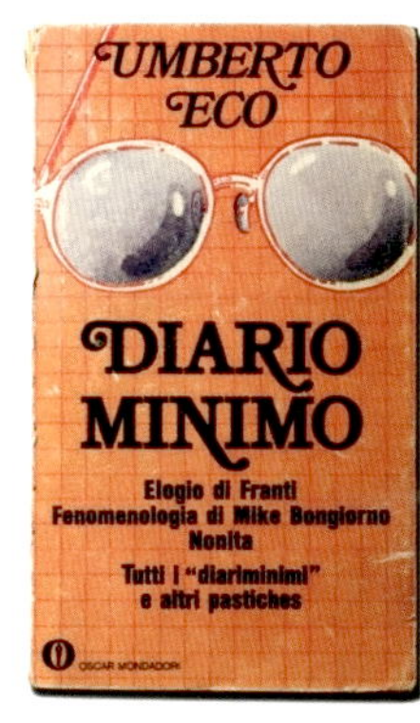

1. Bandoneon; 2. CDs by Akkura, a band from Palermo; 3. Umberto Eco's *Diario minimo*, one of Simone's favourite books.

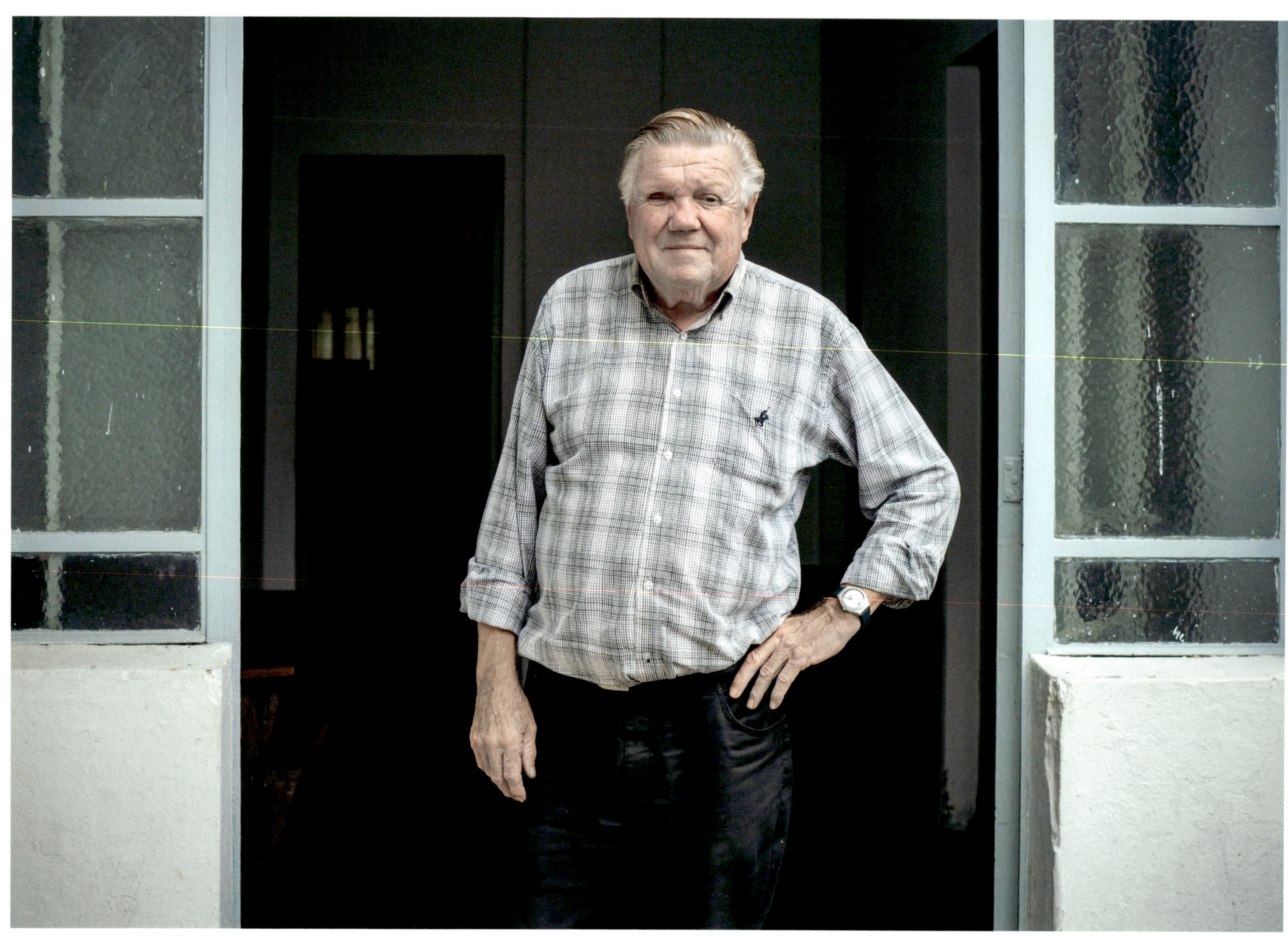

Cesar Toffolo was born in San Donà del Piave (Treviso). In 1952, still only a young boy, he moved to La Plata together with his mother Antonia to join his father Riccardo, who had emigrated a few years earlier. One of the most emotional moments of his life was returning to San Donà del Piave after many years and revisiting the places of his childhood. La Plata (Argentina) 2016.

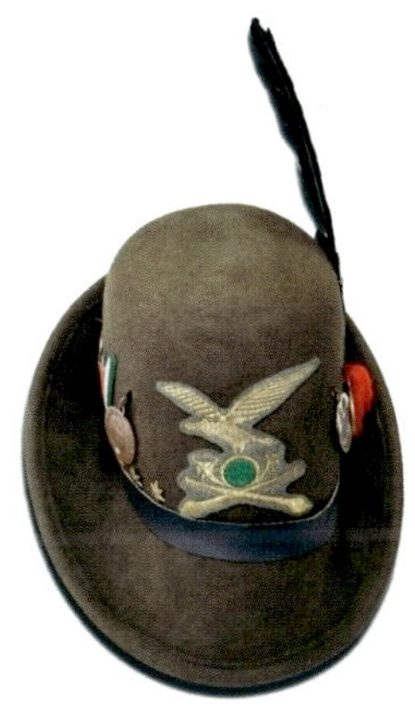

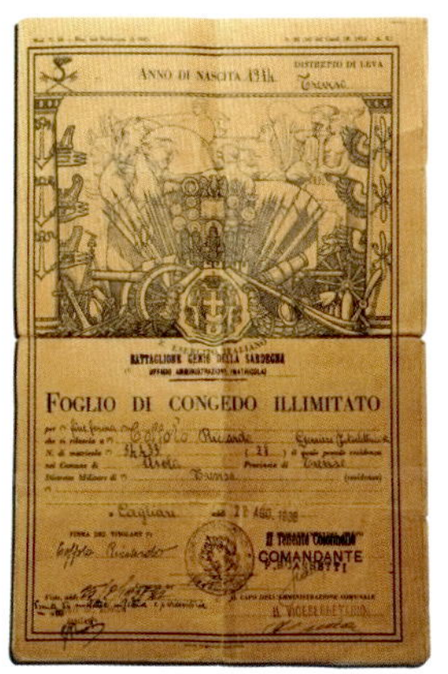

ANNO DI NASCITA 1914

DISTRETTO DI LEVA

FOGLIO DI CONGEDO ILLIMITATO

COMANDANTE

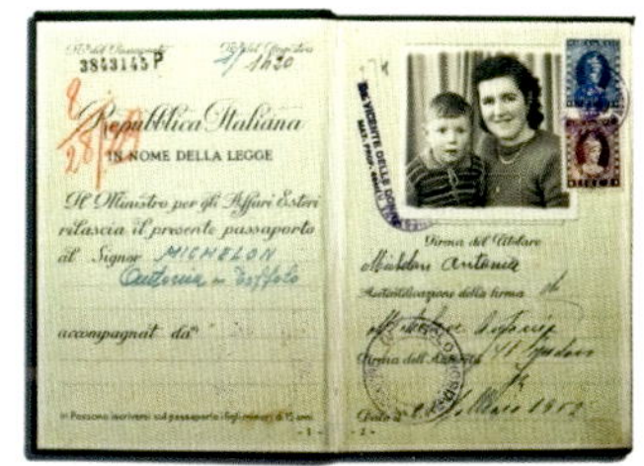

Repubblica Italiana

IN NOME DELLA LEGGE

Il Ministro per gli Affari Esteri rilascia il presente passaporto al Signor

1. and 2. *Alpino* (Italian Alpine Soldier) hat and authorized leave certificate; 3. Travel document obtained for the journey of Cesar and his mother.

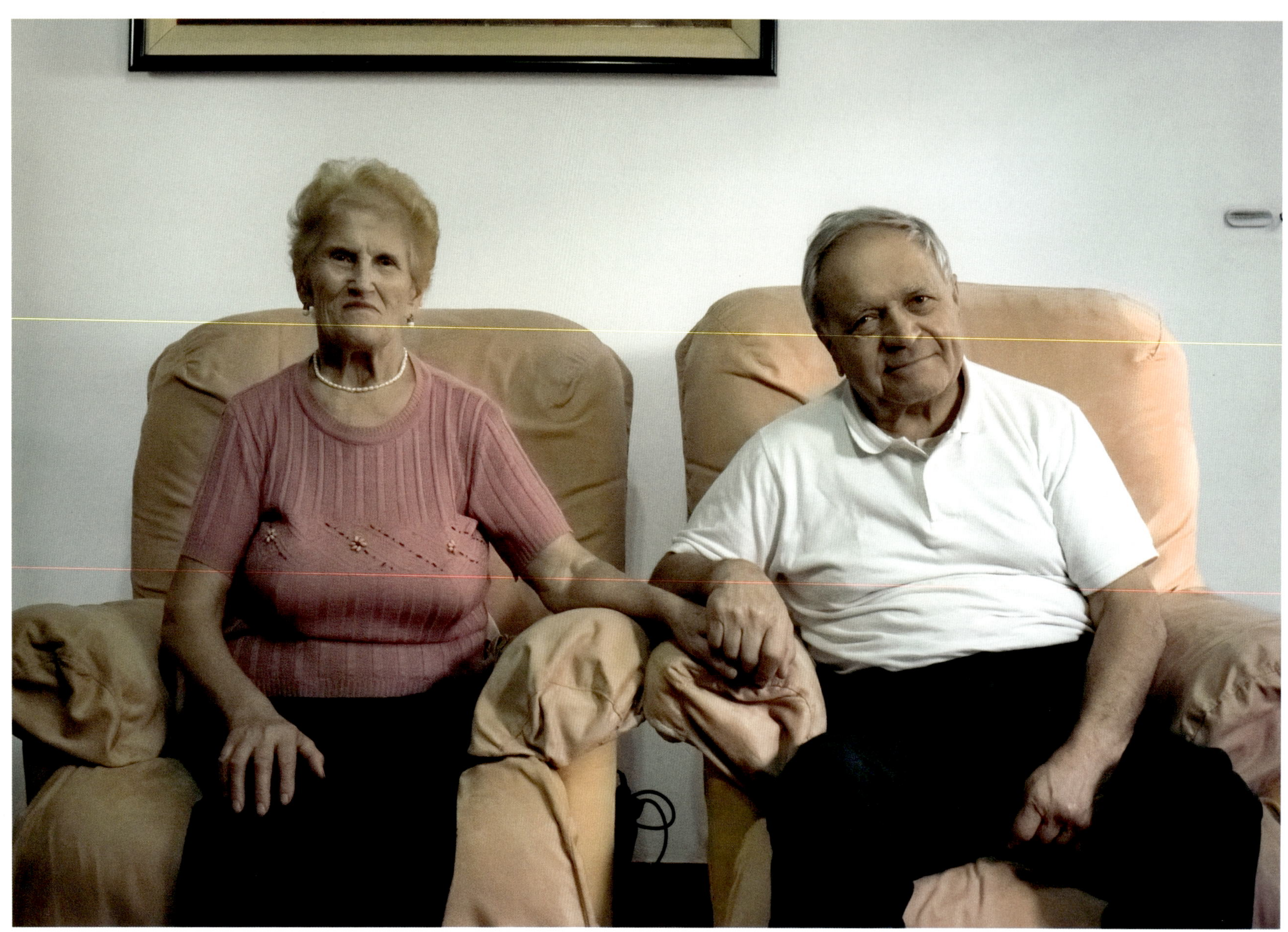

Domenico Marraffini and Filomena Bolgona are originally from Carpineto Sinello in Abruzzo. In 1947, Domenico's father moved to Belgium where he started work in the mines. After working for two years in the mines, he decided to move to Argentina (Domenico was 16 when he left Belgium). In 1956, nineteen-year-old Filomena from Carpineto was offered to him in an arranged marriage. In the following years, Domenico and Filomena became militant communists and founded a mutual aid society for Italians. Ensenada (Argentina) 2016.

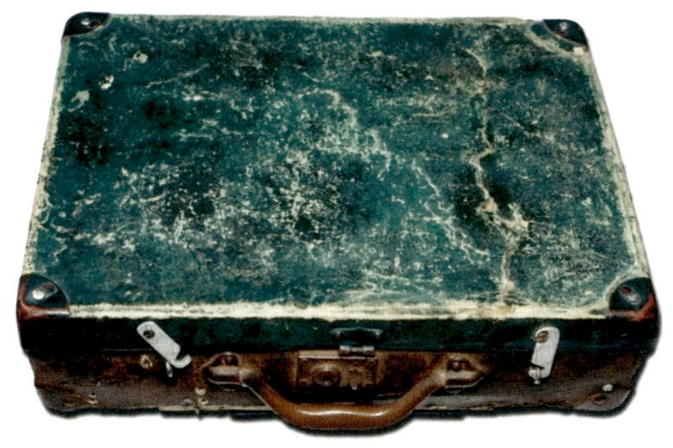

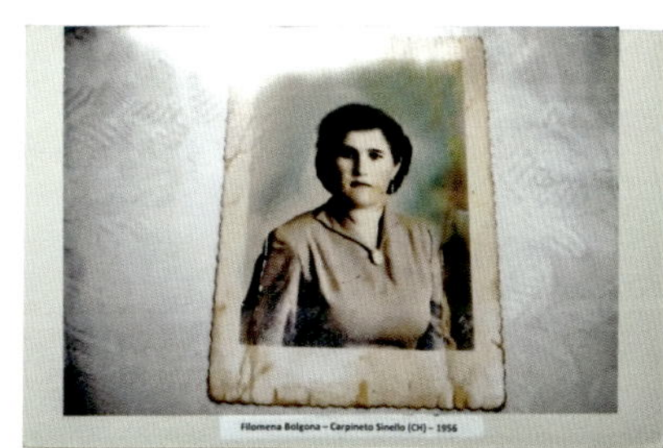

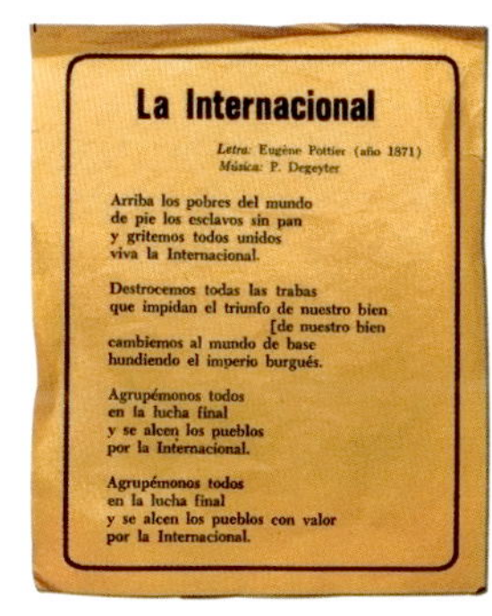

La Internacional

Letra: Eugène Pottier (año 1871)
Música: P. Degeyter

Arriba los pobres del mundo
de pie los esclavos sin pan
y gritemos todos unidos
viva la Internacional.

Destrocemos todas las trabas
que impidan el triunfo de nuestro bien
[de nuestro bien
cambiemos al mundo de base
hundiendo el imperio burgués.

Agrupémonos todos
en la lucha final
y se alcen los pueblos
por la Internacional.

Agrupémonos todos
en la lucha final
y se alcen los pueblos con valor
por la Internacional.

1. Old suitcase containing family photographs; 2. Domenico requested a photograph of Filomena for their engagement – she sent him a photograph of the original image; 3. Spanish translation of 'The Internationale'.

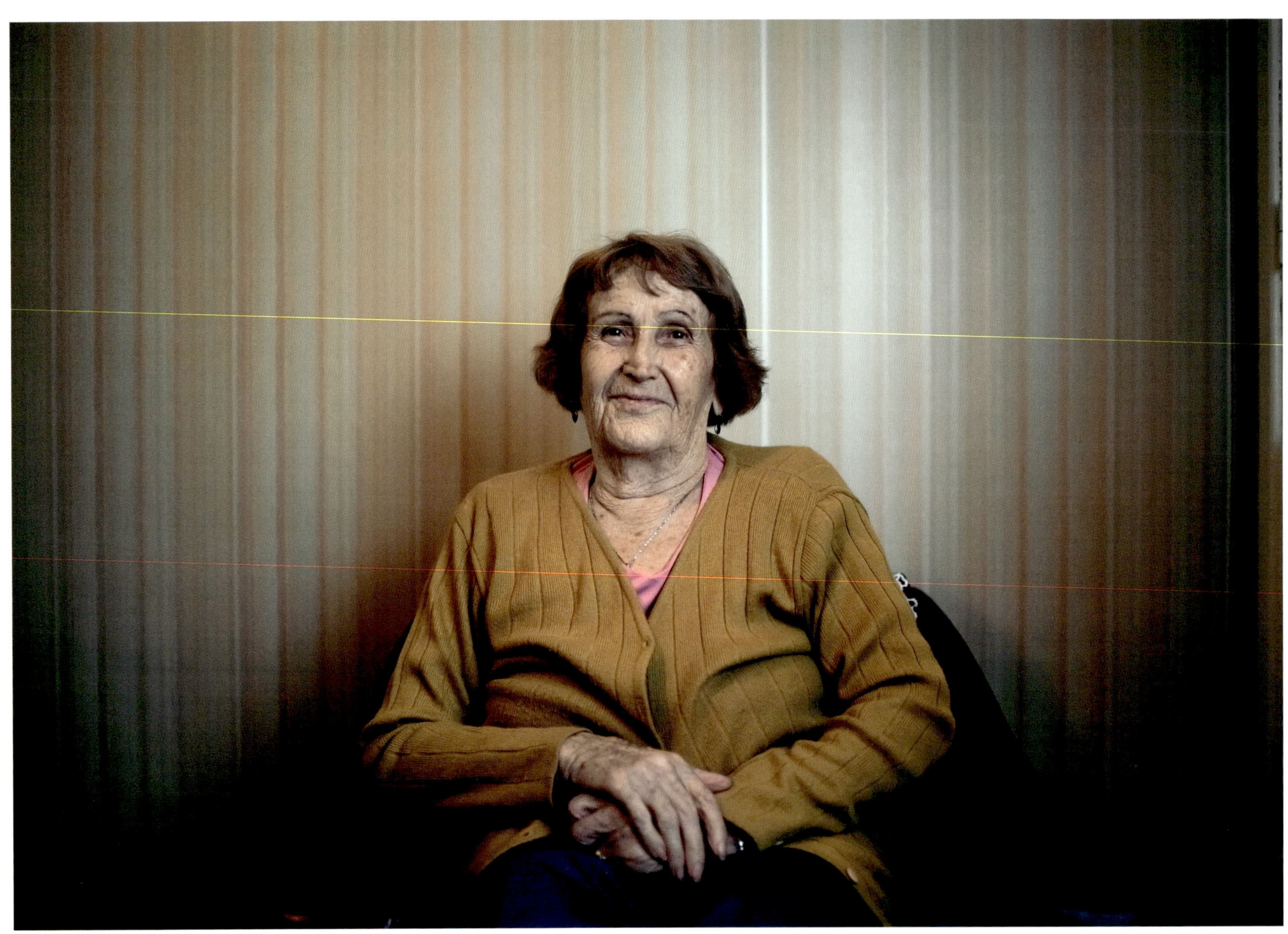

Elsa Gasparinetti's husband Bruno was a sailor in the Italian navy and served in the Second World War. He later decided to move to Argentina, where his sister already lived with her family – they had moved in the 1920s. Bruno began working on the trams, and also sold fabric. On the 11 October 1949, he was reunited with Elsa and their daughter Wilma after they had made the two-week journey to Argentina on the ship 'Sestriere'. La Plata (Argentina) 2016.

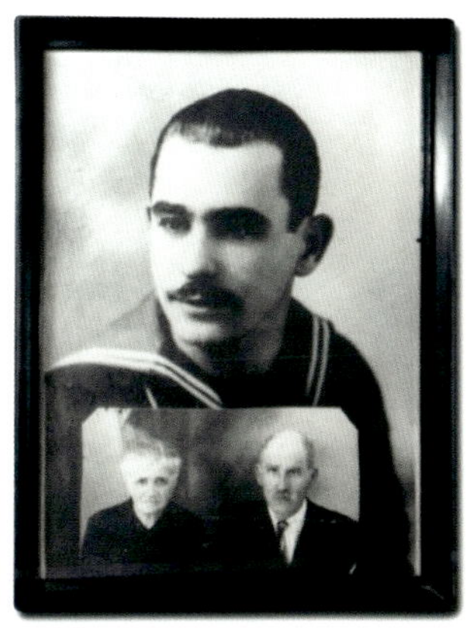

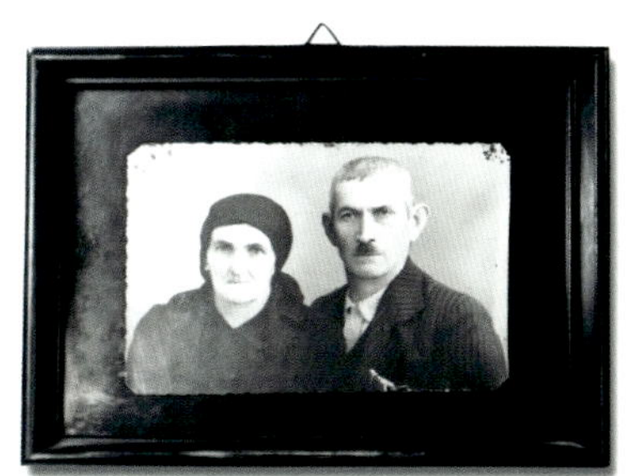

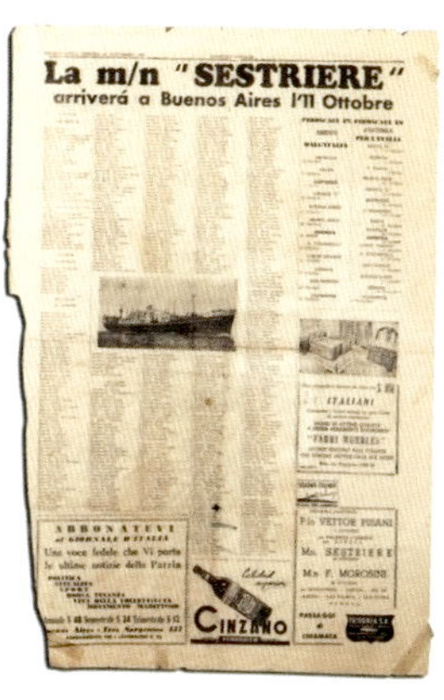

La m/n "SESTRIERE"
arriverá a Buenos Aires l'11 Ottobre

ABBONATEVI
Una voce fedele che Vi porta le ultime notizie della Patria

CINZANO

P/o VETTOR PISANI
M/n SESTRIERE
M/n F. MOROSINI

1. Photo of Elsa's husband Bruno and his parents; 2. Photo of Elsa's parents; 3. Newspaper with the passenger list of the 'Sestiere' (including the names of Elsa and Vilma) dated 11 October 1949, the day of their arrival in Argentina.

NOTES ON CONTRIBUTORS

Mario Badagliacca is a freelance Sicilian photographer. He studied International Relations and Politics at the University of Naples 'L'Orientale', and photo-reportage and photojournalism in Rome. Along with his photographic activity, he has always collaborated with non-profit organizations, and been involved in humanitarian programmes. His work documents migration, life on the borders, human right violations, and social issues.

Charles Burdett is Professor of Italian at the University of Durham. His main areas of research are literary culture under Fascism, travel writing, the Italian colonial presence in Libya and east Africa and its legacy, theories of intercultural contact and the representation of Islam and the Islamic world in recent Italian literature and culture. He was principal investigator of the collaborative research project 'Transnationalizing Modern Languages: Mobility, Identity and Translation in Modern Italian Cultures' (2014–17). He is currently Director of the Institute of Modern Languages Research at the School of Advanced Study, University of London.

Luci Callipari-Marcuzzo is an Italian Australian multi-disciplinary artist, mother, researcher, arts worker, curator, and writer. Based near Mildura in north west Victoria, Australia, her practice-based research investigates, interprets, and translates the experiences of Calabrian Italian women settlers to north west Victoria in a contemporary visual art and sociological context.

Jacopo Colombini holds a PhD in Italian Studies from the University of St Andrews. His research interests range from critical migration studies, to post-colonial theory, transnationalism and memory studies. Currently, he is responsible for the development of an intercultural helpdesk for refugees with disabilities for a German NGO. During his work in the AHRC funded 'Transnationalizing Modern Languages' project, he focused on the transnational symbolism of Lampedusa. His book *Transnational Lampedusa. Representing migration in Italy and beyond* will be published with Palgrave Macmillan in 2023.

Derek Duncan is Professor of Italian at the University of St Andrews. He has published extensively on modern Italian culture, particularly on intersections of gender/sexuality and of race/ethnicity in a transnational framework. He is increasingly engaged with developments in the creative humanities and in the fusion of academic research and creative practice.

Donna R. Gabaccia is Professor of History, Emerita, at the University of Toronto. She is the author and editor of many books and articles on Italian migration around the world. Currently she serves as general editor of the Cambridge History of Global Migrations.

Born in Sicily, Edvige Giunta is the author of *Writing with an Accent: Contemporary Italian American Women Authors* and co-editor of several anthologies. Her non-fiction and poetry have appeared in *Creative Nonfiction*, *Tiny Essays*, *Barrow Street*, *100-Word Story*, *Mutha Magazine*, and other publications. She is Professor of English at New Jersey City University.

Margaret Hills de Zárate's background is in art and art therapy with a particular interest in forced migration and ethnography. She is an Honorary Senior Lecturer at QMU, Edinburgh and a visiting lecturer at the Autonoma University of Barcelona. Margaret lives in Rome where she is working with colleagues from Berlin and Palermo as an editor on a series of books focussing on the arts therapies and the mental health of children and young people.

Shirin Ramzanali Fazel is a bilingual writer. Her publications include the novels *Far from Mogadishu* (2013), *Clouds Over the Equator. The Forgotten Italians* (2017), and the collections of poems *Wings* (2018) and *I Suckled Sweetness* (2020). With Simone Brioni she co-wrote the scholarly text *Scrivere di Islam. Raccontare la diaspora* (2020).

Barbara Spadaro is Lecturer in Italian History and Culture at Liverpool University. The principal areas of her research are history and memory of colonialism, whiteness and migration between Italy and North Africa. Her most recent publication, with Charles Burdett and Loredana Polezzi, is the edited volume *Transcultural Italies: Memory, Mobility and Translation* (2020).

Nicoletta Vallorani is Professor of English Literature and Cultural Studies at the University of Milan. Her research focuses on visual and post-colonial studies, with specific reference to migration in the Mediterranean. She has recently published on crime fiction and migration studies (*Postcolonial Crime*, 2014), and Conrad and imperialism (*Nessun Kurtz*, 2017). She co-authored with Simona Bertacco the volume on translation and migration *The Relocation of Culture* (2021).

Georgia Wall is an Italian to English translator. She has been awarded a mentorship as part of the National Centre for Creative Writing Emerging Translator Programme (2020–21) and is currently translating a contemporary Italian young adult novel. She is also an Italian language tutor at the University of Warwick.